RADICAL HOPE

RADICAL HOPE

Letters of Love and Dissent in Dangerous Times

Edited by Carolina De Robertis

Vintage Books
A Division of Penguin Random House LLC
New York

This is precisely *the time when artists go to work. . . .*
We speak, we write, we do language. That is how
civilizations heal.

—TONI MORRISON, "No Place for Self-Pity,
No Room for Fear," *The Nation*, March 23, 2015

Contents

RADICAL HOPE

A SYMPHONY OF VOICES

Carolina De Robertis

Dear Reader,

Three days after the 2016 election, I sat at my writing desk overwhelmed by grief. I was not alone. Like many people (like you, perhaps), I'd had trouble sleeping, and had already engaged in many conversations—with friends and family, students and colleagues, in person and on social media— about the spike in hate crimes, the pain and outrage, the devastation to come.

In my grief, I thought about many things. I thought about all the hard-won civil rights gains of the past fifty years, now under a new level of threat. I thought about the many communities—including immigrants, people of color, gay and transgender people, women, Muslims, Jews, progressives from all walks of life—now bracing themselves (or ourselves, for I belong to some of those groups) for an era of increased vulnerability. I thought about climate change. The Supreme Court. Democracy. Other nations, affected, watching. The future near and far.

I thought about a friend's daughter, age seven, Black, born in the USA, who said she was scared that Trump would make her family leave the country. And another friend's son, age four, who has two mothers, just as my children do; he asked whether their family would be torn apart.

I thought about my son, who was born days after Obama was first inaugurated, and had therefore always lived in a nation in which someone like him—Black and multiracial, child of an immigrant—could be president. For months, my son had been talking about using his kung fu skills to defend his Mexican friends from Trump and his wall. On November 9, he did not want to get out of bed for school, because, he said, he refused to set foot in a nation where Trump was president. It was not an act of fear; it was a boycott.

I thought about my four-year-old daughter's words about Trump, spoken out of the blue: "We're not beautiful to him. Nobody told me that. It's just a feeling I have."

I also thought about my grandmother, a poet and activist in Uruguay who died during the dictatorship. Born in Argentina, exiled under President Juan Perón (who, it must be pointed out, was not a dictator but a democratically elected authoritarian), she found refuge in the calm little nation of Uruguay, only to later watch both her native and adopted countries fall prey to military coups and reigns of terror, imprisonment, disappearances, and torture. Her later, unpublished poems, found in her house after she died, speak to the depths of her sorrow. She never had the chance to see those dictatorships lift. I wondered how she'd managed to get through each day, to stay alive inside, to keep fighting in the face of repression, to keep the faith, to take the long view. And I wondered about hope. Had she been able to retain any hope? Could she ever have imagined that, years later, in 2010, two of the brutally tortured political prisoners of the Uruguayan dictatorship would rise up to become the beloved president and First Lady of the nation? That José Mujica and Lucía Topolansky would preside over an era of unprecedented renewal and progressive change? In the thick of the bleak times, how could she have imagined such a future? How could she have imagined that the seeds of a bright future lay right there in the horrific times themselves? If I could go back in time to reach her, what would I say, and what would she, reaching forward toward me where I sat at my writing desk, have to say to me?

I thought about you that morning, though I may not know you personally. I thought about the long journey ahead for you and for me and for all of us, and I wondered what we would do—what we could do, what we must do— to get through these times as intact as possible, keeping sight of the long view, striving to stay sane, awake, engaged, and steadfast in the face of backlash and threats to the communities and values and democracy we hold dear.

With all of that in mind, I started reaching out to writers to ask them to join me in what at first was a rather strange and nebulous concept: a collection of love letters in response to these political times.

Why love letters?

The epistolary essay, or essay in letter form, has unique powers. A potent example, one that inspired this book,

lies in the great James Baldwin's "My Dungeon Shook—
Letter to My Nephew on the One Hundredth Anniversary
of Emancipation," published in *The Fire Next Time* in 1963
(the same year Dr. Martin Luther King, Jr., penned another
seminal and brilliant epistolary essay, "Letter from Birmingham Jail"). Baldwin's letter is addressed to his young
nephew, and it gives voice to the injustices of institutional
racism, the beauty and dignity of Black life, and the need
for social change. The tone is at once tender and analyti-
cal, impassioned and nuanced, sweeping and deeply personal. Baldwin showed us that letter-essays, as a form, are
perfectly situated to blend incisive political thought with
intimate reflections, to fold them into a single embrace.

And that's where the love comes in. Love is the blend-
ing agent that fuses the political and the intimate, providing urgency to one and context to the other. In a letter,
the thoughts at hand are undergirded by the need to connect with the intended recipient—and this spirit of extension beyond oneself can link social themes to our personal
spheres, to what cuts the closest and matters most. It is
love that pushes us to face the journey toward justice without flinching, love that impels us to keep going on the
long, hard road, love that provides the moral compass and
the map.

As for the word *dissent*, it entered this project as an
expression of how these letters defend truth in the face of
repression. As my exiled grandmother could have told you,
it doesn't take a dictator to create an atmosphere of fear and
shut down freedom of speech. All it takes is a bully at the
helm, using threats and intimidation against any journalist

(or former Miss Universe, or *Hamilton* actor, or ordinary citizen) to raise the specter of silence and censorship. And so, in such a climate, we can either silence ourselves and live in fear or we can stand ever taller and speak. Dissent is verbal resistance. It is the affirmation of our voices, of our worth. It is, in a democracy, a fundamental right. And, in fact, dissent is not unrelated to love. They are complementary forces. In a climate where bigotry is an explicit value of those in institutional power, speaking love is an act of dissent.

The responses to my call for letters stunned me—with their generosity, their depth, their keen insights and raw sense of urgency. I could not be more moved or humbled by the authors whose words are gathered here: They are leading novelists, journalists, poets, activists, and political thinkers. They are a collective mirror of precisely what makes this society strong and beautiful. They are members of diverse communities with roots all over the world—hailing from Syria, Lebanon, Mexico, Cuba, Nigeria, China, Japan, Egypt, India, Puerto Rico, Iran, Guatemala, indigenous North America, Russia, and various parts of Europe and Africa—and they all claim the United States as home. They are neighbors and activists, professors and artists, mothers and fathers, sons and daughters, straight and gay and transgender. They are Jews and Muslims, Christians and Buddhists, atheists and people undeclared in their spirituality. Above all, they are concerned citizens and community members who care deeply about their country and are compelled to offer their voices in the service of justice, courage, and radical hope.

Each in their own way, these brave, bold writers take the measure of what's been lost with this shift in our society, what's changed and what hasn't, where we are now, and what this means for the road forward on both intimate and societal levels. Among other topics, they explore the struggles, triumphs, and migrations that have shaped their lives and the fabric of this nation; the will to go on when one is depleted or discouraged; the profound lessons to be drawn from ancestors who taught ingenuity in the face of poverty, or spoke out powerfully against slavery, or kept the indigenous ways of the land; what could or should happen next for progressives or for the Democratic Party; the political battles ahead; the quiet inner battles for hope and resilience that form the unsung heart of any movement for a better world; the forces that keep us connected; daring visions for future generations, and road maps for bringing them to birth; the inner sources of fuel that spur us on to work and dream and plan and write and read and speak and care and shape our world as best we can, despite the challenges, for ourselves, for each other, for those yet to come.

There will be many books written about the Trump era from a single author's point of view, and there's no question that many of those books will be invaluable. I look forward to reading and learning from them. At the same time, it's my belief that the challenges of this era also call for a multivocal response, as there are truths about this moment that can only be fully expressed through the prismatic proliferation of voices. In other words, no soloist can fully capture the music of our times; we also need symphonies. Because there are many truths, many ways of knowing, many perspectives from which these times are experienced, and it is precisely this dazzling range that gives our voices power and makes our coalition, still, unstoppably, an ascendant majority in this country and the world.

I have arranged these letters and essays into a loosely woven narrative arc, divided into three parts: "Roots" explores the histories that bring us to this moment, with many letters addressed to ancestors; "Branches" addresses present-day people or communities—a stranger in the supermarket, baby boomers, millennials, white people, artists, the protestors at Standing Rock—and delves into complex questions of our current era; and, finally, "Seeds" looks to the future by speaking to new generations, to sons and daughters, to godchildren, or to imagined children yet to be born, all of them inheritors of what happens now.

I call these sections loosely woven because, indeed, each essay is a microcosm of thought, a fully formed world, and, therefore, can be read in any order, or as a stand-alone piece in its own right. There's no one right way to approach this book. The themes in these letters rise and fall with their own rhythm, overlapping and echoing as they will. And this is as it should be. There is no seed without branches, no branch without roots, no growth of new roots without seeds.

There is great danger in these times. And yet, all is not lost. The future remains unwritten, ours to shape—though it will not be easy. Institutional power has been hijacked by a crew of corrupt, racist, misogynistic, xenophobic, blithely incompetent leaders bent on dismantling the very hallmarks of this nation's democracy. We need to be in a sustained and continuous state of resistance, for as long as it takes, in order to protect our collective rights and the future of the planet. This is hard work. One could easily become exhausted, or paralyzed by despair. That is where this book comes in. There is an antidote to despair to be found in connection, in shared words and thoughts and voices. I invite you to find, in these pages, whatever you most need: a balm, a salve, a rallying cry, a lyrical manifesto, a power source, a mirror, a sanctuary, a hand to hold, a beacon, a torch to light the way.

It is my hope that the words gathered here will lift you, feed you, shake you awake, offer insight, and help you to feel less alone. They are here for you, a steady refuge. They are full of exquisite courage and profound truths about this moment in the great narrative we call human history, sung in many voices, with the heart as well as the intellect ablaze.

It's all here. We're all here. And we will continue to be here. We are the majority, dear reader, the future is ours, and we are in this together.

Con mucho amor,

Carolina
Oakland, California
Martin Luther King, Jr., Day, January 16, 2017

RADICAL HOPE

Junot Díaz

Querida Q.:

I hope that you are feeling, if not precisely better, then at least not so demoralized. On Wednesday, after he won, you reached out to me, seeking advice, solidarity. You wrote, *My two little sisters called me weeping this morning. I had nothing to give them. I felt bereft. What now? Keep telling the truth from an ever-shrinking corner? Give up?*

I answered immediately, because you are my hermana, because it hurt me to hear you in such distress. I offered some consoling words, but the truth was I didn't know what to say. To you, to my godchildren, who all year had been having nightmares that their parents would be deported, to myself.

I thought about your e-mail all day, Q., and I thought about you during my evening class. My students looked rocked. A few spoke about how frightened and betrayed they felt. Two of them wept. No easy task to take in the fact that half the voters—neighbors, friends, family—were willing to elect, to the nation's highest office, a toxic misogynist, a racial demagogue who wants to make America great by destroying the civil rights gains of the past fifty years.

What now? you asked. And that was my students' question, too. *What now?* I answered them as poorly as I answered you, I fear. And so I sit here now in the middle of the night, in an attempt to try again.

So what now? Well, first and foremost, we need to feel. We need to connect courageously with the rejection, the fear, the vulnerability that Trump's victory has inflicted on us, without turning away or numbing ourselves or lapsing into cynicism. We need to bear witness to what we have lost: our safety, our sense of belonging, our vision of our country. We need to mourn all these injuries fully, so that they do not drag us into despair, so repair will be possible.

And while we're doing the hard, necessary work of mourning, we should avail ourselves of the old formations that have seen us through darkness. We organize. We form solidarities. And, yes: we fight. To be heard. To be safe. To be free.

For those of us who have been in the fight, the prospect of more fighting, after so cruel a setback, will seem impossible. At moments like these, it is easy for even a matatana to feel that she can't go on. But I believe that, once the shock settles, faith and energy will return. Because let's be real: we always knew this shit wasn't going to be easy. Colonial power, patriarchal power, capitalist power must always and everywhere be battled, because they never, ever quit. We have to keep fighting, because otherwise there will be no future—all will be consumed. Those of us whose ancestors were owned and bred like animals know that future all too well, because it is, in part, our past. And we know that by fighting, against all odds, we who had nothing, not even our real names, transformed the universe. Our ancestors did this with very little, and we who have more must do the same. This is the joyous destiny of our people—to bury the arc of the moral universe so deep in justice that it will never be undone.

But all the fighting in the world will not help us if we do not also hope. What I'm trying to cultivate is not blind optimism or inane positivity but what the philosopher Jonathan Lear calls radical hope. "What makes this hope *radical*," Lear writes, "is that it is directed toward a future goodness that transcends the current ability to understand what it is." Radical hope is not so much something you have but something you practice; it demands flexibility, openness, and what Lear describes as "imaginative excellence." Radical hope is our best weapon against despair, even when despair seems justifiable; it makes the survival of the end of your world possible. Only radical hope could have imagined people like us into existence. And I believe that it will help us create a better, more loving future.

I could say more, but I've already imposed enough, Q.: time to face this hard new world, to return to the great shining work of our people. Darkness, after all, is breaking—a new day has come.

Love,

J

Roots

DEAR MAMA HARRIET

Alicia Garza

Dear Mama Harriet,

You were the first person I thought about on November 8, 2016, when they announced that Donald Trump had been elected as the forty-fifth president of the United States. The first time you used the Underground Railroad was in September 1849. Legend has it that once you escaped, you never looked back.

The president at that time, Zachary Taylor, died before he could weigh in on the debate surrounding our humanity. The year he died, Congress passed the Fugitive Slave Act, determined to keep people like you from the promise of America—life, liberty, and the pursuit of happiness. When President Polk had taken office a few years earlier, he apparently considered slavery to be a "side issue," less important than stealing land from Mexico and other economic issues. I imagine you didn't care much about who was elected president then, since they were all slaveholders. But you did care about politics.

The truth is I think about you often. Your courage in the face of adversity makes it so that I can put one foot in front of the other, even when I'm tired, even when I'm scared, even when I'm not completely sure what I'm doing or if it will work. I think about you in this political moment, where there are times when us Black folk can be our own worst enemies. When someone tells me that it can't be done, that it doesn't fit with what we've always done, I hear you saying to me, "I freed a thousand slaves, and I could have saved a thousand more if only they had known they were slaves."

I work hard to embody you, Mama Harriet. When I learned that after you escaped, your brothers had second thoughts and turned back, but you kept going, it gave me the strength to keep going. When I learned that you went back to bring your husband to freedom, and he refused to come with you, instead electing to stay with his new wife, it gave me the strength to always be my own compass. When I learned that you returned to bring your sister to freedom and found out that she had since died, it gave me the determination to keep going, though we may never know the outcome of what we do or whether our goals will actually be accomplished.

Mama Harriet, I wonder what sustained you after all of the heartbreak and disappointment that you endured. I wonder how you kept going. I imagine it was ancestors to you, as you are to me, that kept you steady and focused, soothed your heart when it felt like it was shattered into a million pieces, gave you visions of what freedom could be, gave you courage, and infused you with a deep love for your people, whether or not they always loved themselves.

Mama Harriet, when they passed the Fugitive Slave Act, you were undeterred. You simply moved the Underground Railroad to a place more favorable for success, because that's how committed you were. You didn't quit. You didn't give up. Every opportunity for freedom guided your decisions. You weren't afraid to work with anyone who shared the same goal, even if they didn't share your experience. You worked with abolitionists like John Brown, you worked with Quakers, you worked with suffragettes—even when they couldn't see your humanity. You were the first woman to lead an assault at Combahee River, where you helped to free seven hundred slaves. You broke barriers; you pushed boundaries. I'm sure you had peers who didn't like how powerful you were, but because you stood in your power, I can stand in mine.

Mama Harriet, these are perilous times we are living in. Eight years ago, we elected the first Black president of the United States, Barack Obama. This was a historic moment for Black people in this country, no matter how symbolic. Many felt that the election of Barack Obama signaled that we, as a country, had finally moved beyond race. Many attempted to say that his election was the fulfillment of your dreams, Mama Harriet, and the dreams of so many others who came before us. And yet, with President Obama's election, we continued to see the ravages of institutional and systemic racism.

You see, Mama Harriet, the conundrum that you encountered is the same set of contradictions that we encounter. We had a Black president who often shied away from addressing the nation about the pervasive nature of racism, and yet, he faced racism at every turn. Black folks, by and large, were hesitant to criticize the president, of course, for many reasons—many of us could feel, viscerally, the challenges that he faced as a leader. Mama Harriet, we have moved from one form of slavery to other forms. There are astronomical numbers of us in prisons and jails. Too many of us still do not have the basic things we need to survive. Some of us who do find the means are forced to navigate being one of a few in a sea of white bodies, white norms, white culture—and still too many of us seek white acceptance.

But, Mama Harriet, our people have been rising up. Across gender, generation, immigration status (yes, Black people are all over the world), and sexuality, Black people have been rising up. The last decade has seen Black resistance, and the strongest expression of that resistance has occurred over the last four years. Led by a deep and abiding love for all of humanity, we have worked hard to make sure that the lives of Black people are just as valuable as the lives of others.

There was a backlash. A backlash against the supposed progress that was made. A backlash against having a Black leader of the "free" world. Even though all forty-three presidents before him were white and male, when the forty-fourth president of the United States was Black, there were people in this country who believed that this was an example of how Black people are once again getting undeserved handouts. You see, Mama Harriet, the same sickness that caused people to put other people in chains, rape them, strip them of their humanity, work them to their literal deaths while never allowing them to benefit from the fruits of their labor still exists today. Today, the whips are invisible, but the scars remain.

That backlash that I was just telling you about? The result was a president who is unfit to be a leader. A president who was raised in white supremacy, who still embraces it. A president who has no vision for freedom, for justice for all of us. His vision, Mama Harriet, is that he and his friends will continue to get rich off of our backs. Carrots for some, sticks for us, Mama Harriet. The whole system of democracy is in question today, Mama Harriet. There are too many of us who do not believe in democracy anymore. You know what the white folks say, Mama Harriet. They say we don't deserve to make decisions over our own lives. They expect us to just go along to get along. In the same way that the president when you were here with us saw slavery as a "side issue," there are still too many in our society who continue to see race and racism as a "side issue," who instead privilege economic stability over a society where all of us can be all of who we are, all of the time.

Mama Harriet, I'm terrified. I worry every day that none of it is enough. I worry that my heart will harden. I worry that I will lose faith in us. Those feelings are fleeting. I know they will go away. But my real fear? My real fear is that we won't get it together until it's too late. Already, Mama Harriet, the planet is in trouble. The trees and streams and animals that you knew have long since been used up in irresponsible ways. They've poisoned families in Flint, Michigan, Mama Harriet, because when it comes to poor people, when it comes to poor Black people, they say it's okay to drink water laden with lead. This is why I pray to you every day, Mama Harriet. Because I need your strength, your resolve, your courage, and your vision.

Each day I pray to you, Mama Harriet, to give me and all of us the strength to keep moving toward freedom. I know it won't be easy, so I pray that you fortify me and the rest of us. I pray that you help us see slavery clearly so that we can fight it and end it once and for all. I pray that you remove the barriers between us that keep us from being effective together. I pray that you mend our hearts when we break them and when our fight shatters our hearts into a thousand pieces.

And most of all, Mama Harriet, I pray that you are proud of us.

With love,
Alicia

THE LANTERN

Roxana Robinson

To my great-great-great-aunt Hattie, Harriet Beecher
Stowe,

I've been thinking about you a lot recently, Aunt Hattie,
because it seems that we are living in dark times again. I've
been wondering about how you thought about those times,
and how it was that you decided to speak out.

When you wrote *Uncle Tom's Cabin*, it was 1851, and
America had been bringing enslaved people to its shores
for more than two hundred years. So slavery was already
deeply rooted and entrenched; it was a part of our culture.

But it wasn't something you grew up with. You were
born in 1811 in Litchfield, Connecticut, a place where slavery was rare. When you were in your early twenties, your
father took a teaching job in Ohio, and he moved the family
to Cincinnati, which was just across the river from Ken-
tucky. There you became vividly aware of what was happening: you had a front-row seat to the horrifying American

drama of enslaved people trying to escape into freedom. You became an abolitionist. You married Calvin Stowe, a minister who shared your views. When you and Calvin and your brother Henry (my great-grandfather, another abolitionist minister) learned that a family servant was an escaped slave, you helped her to get away to Canada, and to freedom. You became part of the Underground Railroad.

In the early 1850s, you moved to Maine, where Calvin became a professor at Bowdoin. You were no longer close to the misery of slavery, but you couldn't forget it. You were commissioned to write some sketches showing what slavery was really like. What you wrote became *Uncle Tom's Cabin*, one of the most widely read books of the nineteenth century. It changed the way many white people thought about slavery. It roused compassion, which is the opposite of rage.

Rage was an essential part of slavery.

Rage allows us to forget our own humanity. Without rage, we will recognize another person as like ourselves. It's hard to hurt someone you're not angry at; it's anger that drives the impulse to harm. Rage declares itself through violence, and violence was the platform on which slavery was built.

We feel rage when we feel separate; we feel compassion when we feel connected.

What troubled me about our recent election was the way rage seeped into the conversation. I volunteered in a poverty-burdened city in Pennsylvania, and there I heard people raging at the woman candidate for president. Rage erupted at the very mention of her name, as though, just by her existence, she was committing a wrong.

This rage was familiar. I've been the target of that rage because I'm a woman. I've seen it directed at other women and at people who are different in some way.

Having rage directed at you simply because of who you are evokes a strange feeling of helplessness. You stand listening to this outpouring, and you can feel your heart beating in your chest, just as you know the heart is beating in the chest of the person who is enraged. You know that the two of you share this steady internal pulse. And you know that you share something else, too, because you can look into the eyes of that person and see something deep and visceral—you see that you are both human, you each have a soul—and yet the shouts of anger are denying this. The shouts claim that you don't share this sameness, that the two of you are different. They claim that you, yourself, are wrong in your very being.

This claim will still and silence you.

If you are wrong in your being, then nothing you can do will matter. It doesn't matter what you say or write or create or build or sing. In *To the Lighthouse*, Lily Briscoe thinks of the unspoken criticism by Charles Tansley, fellow houseguest: "Women can't paint." It's just that simple, it seems. The fact of your identity defines your capabilities. The angry or contemptuous shouts declare that nothing you do can make a difference. You want to speak up to say this is not true, but you hear the anger, and you understand that nothing you say can change that.

I heard that anger in Pennsylvania. As one young volunteer walked away from a voter's house, a man in the next yard yelled to ask if she was there to campaign for Hillary. He didn't use Hillary's name, though. He called her "that bitch." He was holding a shotgun, in case his message was not clear. It was one of rage and violence.

His fury was directed at a woman who dared to run for president, who dared to claim political power. His rage was directed at people who are different from him—whose skins are another color, or whose religion is unfamiliar— and who dare to claim a place in our society. I heard rage directed at a woman who represented the person I am, just because we are women.

Those feelings of rage and denial are shocking to me. Tolerance is part of our national bedrock, part of our moral foundations: "We hold these truths to be self-evident, that all men are created equal." That's our country's most fundamental premise; it's what we started out with. It means that if we believe in America, we believe in tolerance.

Aunt Hattie, you were shocked by what you saw around you. You felt a moral outrage at the fact of slavery, and you made your outrage known. You raised your voice.

"I wrote what I did because as a woman, as a mother, I was oppressed and broken-hearted with the sorrows and injustice I saw," you said, "because as a Christian I felt the dishonor to Christianity—because as a lover of my country, I trembled at the coming day of wrath."

As lovers of our country, and after a dubious election, bedeviled by malicious meddling, we may feel like you— brokenhearted. We have watched a man who did not win the popular vote, and who seems frighteningly blind to the country's moral core, take his place in our highest office. He was supported by people who were full of anger, who felt forgotten. They saw no way forward. They were losing power, and they saw a woman rising up to take power over them. They felt threatened and enraged. They voted against the woman who dared to claim power, in support of the man who made it feel right to hate that woman.

Rage and hatred are not the engines we want to drive the country, but rage drove those voters, just as rage drove the people who supported slavery.

We know it when we see it.

Looking into the eyes of someone who hates you is diminishing. Who are you, if your being is denied? How can you be human if you are hated? Hatred itself is silencing. Hatred denies us the power of conversation, of exchanging thoughts. If you hate me, we can't speak to each other. We are each alone. If you look at me with rage, you will not know me. You will not believe in the beating of my heart.

The people who hated our candidate would tell you that they hate her because they don't trust her, not because she's female. Secessionists would have told you they were defending states' rights, not slavery. It's possible that these people don't understand the sources of their rage. The people who used brutality to enforce slavery, and the man who carried a rifle to frighten a campaign volunteer, are people who feel doubly threatened. They are threatened by the loss of their own power and of their own humanity.

We women can feel their hatred leveled at us. We understand what it means to be looked at by someone who will not see your soul within your eyes. It feels like a blotting out.

It's a strange idea, this hatred of women, because it means hatred of half the human race. It includes these peoples' own mothers, their wives, their sisters. In Pennsylvania, a volunteer knocked on a door that was opened by a young man. She asked if a certain woman lived there. "Yeah, she does," the young man said. "That's my mother. And you can't talk to her. She's not leaving the house today."

The day on which her son was keeping his mother inside was Election Day. Maybe he didn't trust her alone in the voting booth.

I can feel his anger, a leaping, crowding, tumultuous rage, like the rising tide against the rocks. These people are enraged by us, by the very idea of us.

But they cannot crush us.

As women, we are endowed with certain kinds of potency, and one of them is the power to teach our children. We will influence the next generation. We can teach small people to respect their mothers, share power with their wives, encourage their daughters to understand their strength.

We can do other things, too, of course: we can run for office, found companies, solve theorems, design bridges, treat illnesses, write books, star in movies. We can stand up and speak out. This is the way forward: through raising our voices.

So, Aunt Hattie, like you, I will set down my thoughts. I will make known the fact that I defy intolerance, that I believe in democracy. That I treasure our beautiful planet, our tumultuous seas, our brilliant birds, our great mammals, our fragile butterflies. I'll write that I value fairness and kindness and equality. I'll say that we must meet the eyes of another human being, whether or not that person looks like us. That we must hear every heart as it beats.

Those who are angry are letting that tide separate themselves from their own mothers, their wives and daughters.

We are those people. It's up to us to decide not to let that rage hurt us. We can make ourselves impermeable. We can choose not to let their thoughts define ours.

Aunt Hattie, when you wrote that book, I imagine you were thinking of something radical: the abolition of slavery itself. You were only one small woman, and you were looking up at an enormous edifice, towering and monolithic, but what you wrote made the whole structure start to tremble and shudder, and finally, it all came down, thundering and crashing. It wasn't just because of your book, of course, but your book made it impossible for people to think of slavery in the old way.

So right now, as we are fumbling our way through the dimness, I think of you, setting down your thoughts and speaking out.

Slavery, you said, is an abomination.

We can speak out now ourselves and say that rage at others is an abomination, rage at women, blacks, Asians, Muslims, LGBTQ—all the groups of others that include us, whoever we are.

We are here, we women, and we will always be here. We will always be watching, and we will always be ready to meet your eyes. We will not allow you to define us, nor our thoughts, nor our children, nor our government. We will stand up and speak out, as we always have in this country, as we always will. We will be steadfast, and our hearts will always beat like yours. When you are ready to see us, and to see our souls, we will be here, ready to meet your gaze.

There are the dark hours, and then there is the coming of the light. Aunt Hattie, thank you for your lantern.

Roxana Robinson
Litchfield County, Connecticut
December 21, 2016

DEAR HENRY

Lisa See

Dear Henry,

I don't ever want you to feel hopeless or powerless. Now, of course, you have the usual ways that little boys can feel hopeless and powerless—bedtime, for example—but I'm talking about bigger things. You paid surprising attention to the election. How could you not when your parents, your uncle, Grandpa, and I were talking about it *all the time*? When we were out to breakfast, the conversation might be about the rise of neo-Nazism, the possible defunding of Planned Parenthood, women's rights in general, the dismantling of the Affordable Care Act, our criminal justice system, and targeting people because of the color of their skin, their religion, where they came from, or how they got here. You've also heard us talk about how none of these things will matter if we end up having a nuclear war or go off the deep end when it comes to global climate change. Immediately after the election, you heard us sound hopeless, frightened, or angry. Yep, you saw us freaking out, and I'm sorry about that. You're only four and a half. We should have been more careful.

But here's what I want you to know: We aren't helpless, and things aren't hopeless. We may not work in the Senate or Congress or the White House, but we aren't powerless either. We are strong as a family, and we're strong as individuals. Don't ever think, *I can't fight back*, because you can. Whenever you think, *Oh, this is too hard or too dangerous*, or *Whatever I could do would be too small to make a difference*, I want you to remember the people in your own family who faced variations of what the president-elect and his cronies are threatening. I'm not going to write about your mom's side of the family. That's for them to tell, but I know they have stories of your relatives who showed great courage. And I'm not going to tell you about my mom's side of the family. Instead I'll just focus on my dad's family—in particular your great-great-grandparents Stella and Eddy— who rose up and fought against circumstances that seemed as immutable as stone.

You never met Stella and Eddy, but I did, and they inspire me to this moment. The things you love—or I hope you love—about me come directly from them. I used to spend a lot of time doing chores in the yard with Grandpa Eddy, just as you and I do today. (I'm dreading the day when you realize, *Hey, all she does is make me rake, sweep, dig, clip, and pull weeds*.) Grandma Stella always had special projects just for the two of us, just like you and I have: experimenting with vinegar and baking soda, making forts, exploring. And guess what? My red hair—and the disposition that goes with it—comes from her, too. My grandparents didn't have a lot of money or education, but they were resolute people. They had to be. They were unique for their time, but I believe they would be unique even today.

As you know, you're part Chinese. That doesn't seem like a big deal now, but once upon a time, it was. Excuse me if I digress for a moment to talk about history. In the lead-up to the election of 1876, swing votes were tied to the issue of Chinese immigration in the same way that immigration was a hot topic during this election cycle. Rutherford Hayes endorsed Chinese exclusion and won the election. In the following election, James Garfield also carried the torch of anti-Chinese immigration into office. (From those days to now, *every* presidential election has fanned the flames of anti-immigration. This, Henry, shows that hate and fear are reliable, predictable, and effective political tools.) All this led eventually to the Chinese Exclusion Act of 1882, which barred the entry of all Chinese immigrants to the United States except for those who were teachers, students, diplomats, ministers, or merchants. It also declared all Chinese totally ineligible for naturalized citizenship. This clause alone allowed the United States to join Nazi Germany and South Africa as the only nations ever to withhold naturalization purely on racial grounds.

From this one act, many other laws were passed to make life difficult for the Chinese who were here—even if they'd been born in the United States and therefore were citizens. In our state of California, Chinese down to a quarter couldn't marry a white person. (Anti-miscegenation laws targeted Chinese in twenty-eight states. Here in California, the law was overturned in 1948, but people of Chinese descent in some other states had to wait until 1967 to legally marry a white person.) Chinese—also down to a quarter—couldn't own property in California until 1948. And instead of building a wall, the government built an immigration station on Angel Island in the San Francisco Bay. Its purpose was to keep *all* Chinese immigrants *out*. Despite all that, here we are. How did that happen?

Sometimes you like to be mischievous. Sometimes you like to play tricks. That's what our family often had to do just to be in this place you have always known as home. Your great-great-great-grandfather Fong See helped bring in a lot of people as fake business partners under the protected category of "merchants." When he decided to marry a white woman, Ticie Pruett, they went to a lawyer, who drew up a contract for them as though they were forming a partnership. Stella and Eddy went to Mexico to get married. (My dad once got in very serious trouble when he told his elementary school class that his mom and dad weren't legally married.) My mom and dad, your great-grandparents, were only the second couple in our whole extended family to be legally married in the United States. When people in our family wanted to buy land, they traded rugs or other merchandise or asked a friend (and they had to hope he would remain loyal and trustworthy for decades) to buy a house in his name. I'm going to eliminate some of the "greats" here and just say that when Uncle Ray was lucky enough to buy a house in Beverly Hills (he could "pass"), he told his daughters, "*Never* ever tell anyone you're part Chinese." Because if they let that information slip out, they would lose their home and the kids would have to go to a different school.

Perhaps the things that have happened in our family have caused us to have sympathy and empathy for others. If boys want to marry boys or girls want to marry girls, that's a nice thing, because you know just from looking at your own family that people should get to marry whomever they want. I mean, just think about the party we had a few days ago. It was just the immediate family for Christmas tamales. When you looked around the room, you could see a little of everything—white, mixed, black, Chinese, East Indian, Persian. And religions? Let's take a journey around the world for that, too. If people don't like it—and many don't—so what? But if anyone ever tells one of us that we can't marry who we want, or we can't live where we want, or we can't worship where and how we want, I hope you stand right by my side and do whatever it takes to give the people we love our support and protection.

As I said at the beginning, we aren't powerful people. But as the Chinese say, *The collapse of a dam begins with an ant hole*. Your great-great-grandparents Stella and Eddy knew this to be true. They got married when it was against the law. They "bought" a house when it was against the law. And they helped others when *they* faced hardship. And they weren't alone. They had their son—my father and your great-grandfather. They also had Ted. He was Stella's little brother. He was just a couple of years older than my father, and difficult circumstances dictated that he had to live with my grandparents. As a result, Ted and my dad were more like brothers than uncle and nephew. During

World War II when the Japanese were interned, this family of four helped many people. Most Japanese who lived in the West—whether American citizens or not—lost everything: their homes, cars, fields, fishing boats, and all their personal belongings. All they could keep was what they could carry. Think about what that would mean to you, Henry, to have only what you could carry.

Benji Okubo, an artist and one of my grandfather's closest friends, left all of his paintings with my grandparents for safekeeping when he was interned at the Heart Mountain Relocation Center in northwest Wyoming. My grandparents also moved into the home of the Oki family. Yes, the rent was cheap, but Stella and Eddy were also able to take care of the Okis' home and belongings until the end of the war when they were released from the internment camp where they'd been held. These events were terrible for the people who were sent away. Never lose sight of that. But they weren't easy for people—like Stella and Eddy—who helped in the way that ants might when faced with a dam. Neighbors, friends, classmates, and business associates didn't like seeing people *help* those who'd been interned. And quite apart from that, our family was Chinese. During the war, Grandpa Eddy and all our Chinese relatives and friends had to wear pins or armbands that read *I'm not Japanese* or *I am Chinese.* They had to put placards in the windows of their homes, cars, and businesses stating their race as Chinese and not Japanese. Even so, shops were vandalized, and people got beaten. No, not easy at all.

The key to being mischievous, using trickery, or being an ant is: *don't do something stupid.* (I'm pretty sure you know this already.) My father's birthday is on the Fourth of July, and his mom and dad always gave him a birthday party. They liked to decorate the house, just like your mom and dad like to do for your parties. One year, when they were living in the Oki family's house, they decided to decorate the patio with Japanese carp kites. That was super stupid! The neighbors called the FBI, and agents came to the house. After the agents broke up the party, they accused Stella and Eddy of using the kites to signal to Japanese submarines. Boy, were they in trouble! I bet the neighbors were even more suspicious after that. I grew up hearing all these stories from my dad and my grandparents, but I also heard them from Benji Okubo and my aunt Kay, a Japanese American, who coincidentally had also been interned at Heart Mountain and then married Uncle Ted after the war. They all talked about hardship, suffering, and humiliation, but they also taught me a lot about civil disobedience, being kind, opening your heart, and how to take a scary story—FBI agents breaking up your birthday party and accusing your mom and dad of being spies is something I hope never happens to you— and turn it into a funny family tale to be recounted again and again.

Okay, Henry, now for a big leap in time. After 9/11 when some in President Bush's cabinet wanted to round up and incarcerate Muslims in the United States, he pointed to Secretary of Transportation Norman Mineta, who'd been a victim of internment, and said we should not do to others what had been done to Norman and his family. We live in different times now. Your mom and dad don't let you watch television, but let me tell you a little of what you can see and hear these days. Recently on Fox News, one of the president-elect's supporters defended the idea of "creating a registry for immigrants of Muslim countries." On *Meet the Press*, Reince Priebus, the president-elect's chief of staff, said there wouldn't be a registry based on religion, but that the administration would "not rule out anything." I'm relieved that the president-elect finally came out to "disavow and condemn" the white nationalists shouting "Heil Trump" at a meeting in our nation's capital a couple of weeks ago. Our new president and his cabinet haven't taken office yet, so there's a case to be made that we don't know what they actually intend to do. But I'll say this: words matter. A little of this, a little of that, and suddenly you're going down a particular path. A "registry" may sound innocuous enough, but the rounding up of Japanese Americans in the western United States and the rounding up of Jews in Germany began innocuously, too.

In honor of my great-grandfather and grandparents, who fought against discrimination and hate in their own lives, and Aunt Kay, Benji Okubo, the Oki family, and other friends and family—all innocent American citizens—who were interned, let's not let the new president strip civil rights from a whole class of people with no probable cause or due process based solely on their faith, race, ethnicity, or gender. We should all want him to rise to the challenges, show his best nature, and protect all Americans, as he has promised he would. So far, we have yet to see an inkling of any of those things. In fact, just the opposite. Whatever he does, we, as ordinary American citizens, have a responsibility to do our part by being vigilant and helping to defend and protect those who may need it in the months and years to come. Earlier, I said I hoped you would stand by my side. But I want you to know that I'll *always* stand by your side, too. Oh, Henry, we're going to have lots of fun being mischievous, using our best tricks, and marching along together as two ants. Do you want to know who else is going to be with us? Mommy, Daddy, Grandpa, Uncle Chris, and so many more. There's hope and power in that.

I'll always love you, but today, I'm loving you for the courage and forthrightness that I know runs in your veins,

Grandma Lisa

NOT A MOMENT BUT A MOVEMENT

Jewelle Gomez

My dearest Grace A.:

You know the story of my younger years: my parents splitting up when I was two years old and how I dropped through the cracks and was sent to live with my paternal grandparents for several years. I have scattered memories of that period, but the sharpest is about hope. My parents were supposed to visit me periodically; I have a visceral memory of the wait for my father to pull up in his big car in front of his parents' house. The moments when my younger self sat expectantly in the parlor, then moved onto the front porch, straining forward like a puppy, remain my way of measuring hope.

Closing my eyes, I can still remember that comfortable flutter in my chest—anticipation of seeing his car turn the corner after an eight-hour drive, and my father gathering his bulk to emerge in an elegant camel hair coat or stylish Bermuda shorts. The thing I've learned about hope is that it's based in two things: first, anticipation of the remembered and recognized, like the feel of my father's stubble as I threw my arms around his neck and he kissed me. But hope is also grounded in projected possibilities. Embedded in my childish embrace was an unconscious imagining of him at my future college graduation or some professional triumph. Even at eight years old, I knew enough to hope one day I'd be introducing him to the woman who'd become my life partner. That quality of being both real and imagined makes hope so powerful it's almost unstoppable.

So on the fourth stop in my small life, at eight years old, I finally landed with you, my maternal great-grandmother, in your Boston flat on the ragged side of town just before urban renewal completely devastated it. Your Ioway/African American spirit relished being the widow of a Wampanoag, a true New Englander impervious to the poverty and the weather. It was in your dim tenement with no hot water and no central heating that my hope grew bigger. You were seventy-three years old and unknowable to me at eight, but in the subsequent fifteen years, I came to understand your life as a child enduring near starvation on Indian land in Iowa. I recognized your isolation in the New England winters of the 1950s and 1960s, when schools kept trying to teach me that all Native people were dead. I came to rely on your unassailable life force and clear vision of the world as well as your devotion and unquestioned support of me and my ambitions. With little education but an ardent habit of reading and a true internal compass, you navigated and triumphed over municipal bureaucracies in order to receive Aid to Families with Dependent Children to support us.

Your indomitable spirit survived whatever the mainstream culture threw at you, whether it was a malnourishing diet of endless corn as a child or the condescension of my high school guidance counselors. You had seen the worst that the United States had to offer and come through by virtue of determination and perhaps your own hope. Most importantly, you taught that sense of hope and determination to me.

So it was kindled inside of me by a father who usually showed up and a great-grandmother who could not be divested of her sense of humanity. When I was on a book tour last year, I saw a sign in a bookstore in a seaside town in Maine that was carefully drawn with popular symbols of coastal living and these words were entwined: *Hope anchors the soul.* From that childhood that many might call "disadvantaged," I was anchored in the belief that most things are possible.

I knew I lived in a country founded on the murder of the body and the spirit of others. Native American nations were decimated with little regret, Africans fell beneath the same juggernaut, and all of the bloodshed was aided and abetted by practitioners of Christianity who manufactured innumerable ways to glorify Manifest Destiny and slavery. The Founding Fathers thought it easier to subjugate by dehumanizing their prey; their descendants find it easier to subjugate their prey by humanizing and prioritizing corporate entities.

I grew up watching the evening news with you every night, and there we saw those who believed in racial equality have their bones broken by police wielding batons and fire hoses and dogs. We watched schoolchildren be spit on in the 1950s, the 1960s in the South, and the North in the 1970s by those who refused to accept the humanity of Black children. We also saw on the news the seemingly endless rows of flag-draped boxes returning the bodies of young soldiers from the wars in Vietnam and Laos while those whose land they despoiled were called gooks. Still, your survival of the atrocities handed out by the Bureau of Indian Affairs and the indignities wielded by the Massachusetts Department of Welfare was my beacon. I understood your hope came not from some belief in the triumph of good or the kindness of politicians and bureaucrats. Your hope came from within; something inside you harbored and nourished a spark that had not been squelched and would always burn inside you and those you were able to touch. I came to believe that light inside came from the pride of knowing you were part of a long line in history that could survive.

Later, after I moved to New York City and got my degree in journalism, I was terrified of being away from home and called you every day. Your sense of how strong I could be made me strong. One day, I was told by an editor at a local television station that I needn't bother coming in for an interview, because they didn't hire women for the night shift—the prime entry-level spot. I was choked with rage but not despair. Solid reminders of you cascaded through my mind: your stalwart walk as you pulled the cart through the glass-strewn park to get to the overpriced shopping district; you climbing the too-steep step to get into the news van so you could visit me at my job at WGBH-TV; your soft Midwest/New England accent as you cursed someone who crossed you with these strange words: "To Hingham with you!"

Since you passed away, the atrocities continue to pile up on one another: the ostracism of people suffering from HIV; the regular acceptance of the killing of young black people by whites in authority; the acceptance of a prison industrial complex that has no intention of rehabilitating; the dismissal of the plight of the indigent; the laying of pipelines through sacred land; the routine rape and sexual harassment of women on college campuses. The list is long enough to make me feel hopeless . . . yet I don't.

Weeks after the November 8 election—or what I've come to call the Zombie Apocalypse—I think a lot about you and the things you survived and the events we saw together outside our living room window, in the newspaper, on television. I find that, by looking back toward you, I can manage to look forward.

This week I was watching *The Rachel Maddow Show* (you'd love her: she's funny and brilliant and just happens to be a stunning butch), and she was interviewing the outgoing attorney general, Loretta Lynch, about the country's postelection future. The entire show was like a burst of hope so bright I almost had to put on sunglasses. The African American attorney general, prim and plump, sat perched on a barstool talking to a white butch lesbian who has her own national television news show! The event was being recorded in the Stonewall Inn, the site of one of the first places where queer people fought back against police violence! (I was so nervous about being a lesbian in 1969, I hid the tiny newspaper clipping from you.) Simply that the interview was happening made me remember that there are people in the world who are not such egotistical, political careerists as to believe that human rights don't matter.

Then, as if just showing up wasn't enough, Attorney General Lynch spoke a truth that is hard to remember from our short-lived perspective: "History is bigger than one turn of the electoral wheel." During your eighty-eight years on this plane, you saw numerous turns of the wheel, and many of them did not land on a prize. Still, toward the end of your life, you took me in and bestowed not just a roof and clothes and food but the gift of your history and the knowledge that we find hope inside ourselves.

The prevalence of so many modes of communication sometimes mutes that possibility of touching our inner resources. We spend a lot of time on the Internet looking at Facebook, Twitter, Instagram, and so many other sites, searching for the words of others who feel the same way we do. The need to vent is natural, and sometimes the very clever memes and quotes can release a bit of the energy that builds up or pull us up from the mire of the election news here and the generally devastating world news. This electronic outlet does the same for those who don't believe in full human rights: they find their like and crow to each other, whipping up anger and violence. The anonymity of the Web and untrustworthiness of media makes it much easier for people to be crude and demeaning, less likely to remember the good manners their grandmothers may have tried to teach them. We see it with youth in school bullying each other on websites and adult trolls who stalk and harass others just for fun and media outlets that manufacture fake news or simply don't check facts. But sometimes in media, I find essays or quotes that remind me of things you had to say, as if you'd whispered in Attorney General Lynch's ear.

You were just a girl of twenty when Emmeline Pankhurst

coined a slogan for the suffragette movement in 1903, so I don't know if you ever heard it: "Deeds not words." It's so simple, yet still essential today, almost a century later. I need a laugh and camaraderie as much as anyone who recognizes inequities, but words, whether delivered face-to-face or hurled at us through the Twittersphere, are worthless unless they lead us toward action.

When I came to live with you, a social worker decided you had no right to financial support for raising me, since my parents were not dead but in fact lived relatively close by. It was like she'd heard that noxious phrase *welfare queen* and put the crown on your head. I don't know if she thought, *This old woman will just go away*, but you didn't. You muttered, "To Hingham with you," then cut your way through thick and sticky red tape until you could legally adopt me so we could receive the meager support offered by the state. I still see you peering closely through failing eyes at stacks of papers that needed to be signed and notarized until the job was done. Even at eight years old, I knew you were doing something extraordinary that would change my life.

That's what I want to do now: something, anything that will change the life of our nation. Human rights are fragile in the face of full-on assault by capitalist demagogues and white men afraid of losing power; but any of us with memories knows how many horrible things we've survived. We remember the images of those who refused to give up on human rights: people being dragged from stools at lunch counters or standing in front of a line of Chinese tanks or lying down in body outlines in front of the capital or chained to the fence of the White House or being force-fed by officials who didn't believe women should vote. Some of these things we saw together; still you didn't back away from hope.

One of the many things I associate with you is your love of music. You played the piano at least an hour a day and then sang along with the Righteous Brothers and Ella Fitzgerald on the radio. I wish you could see some of the musical theater that I see today as I try to create my own plays, all of which are reminders of our ability to hope. I think you'd like the Broadway musical about one of the country's Founding Fathers, *Hamilton*. It's ironic that a story about the men who set the stage for so many horrible historic events in this country is able to remind us that revolution can be an honorable thing. I attribute that to the show's phenomenal creator, Lin-Manuel Miranda, one of whose lyrics captures something we need to remember now as we feel pulled into a vortex of despair. In the musical, Miranda wrote about the heightened period of the American Revolutionary War, where words are swirling around like motes of dust, and his characters remind each other that this is "not a moment, it's the movement." These are powerful words, and no matter Trump's attempts to co-opt them, they belong to us, to the people. For that moment of fighting and dying in a war, when weeping happens, it's because we need it. It's the same with any social change: we look inside ourselves, look at our pasts, and find what propels us forward into organized action, into a movement.

Remembering the hope I had waiting for my father, I understand that somewhere inside we are all that expectant kid. The difference now is that as adults we can still feel that hope, but we don't have to wait. We can get off the porch and act—go out and create the movement we are hoping for.

Sixty years after you took me into your home, I'm just as grateful that you were there as when, at eight, I came home to you. And I thank you for staying with me now as I find my way through this thick fog of disappointment and fear to get back in touch with my hope. Our salvation is not somewhere out in cyberspace. It's inside us; that's where the deeds begin.

As always,
J

A LETTER TO MY SON

Hari Kunzru

Dear Ryu,

I just dropped you at your preschool and walked home, knowing that I would have to write this letter. I've been putting it off, to be honest. It's upsetting to sit here at my desk and worry about you, the little boy who reluctantly let go of my hand and began to sift through a tub of Legos. What did you decide to build? A house? A car? Somewhere to stay, or something that goes?

This has been a wonderful year for us, because your little sister arrived. Your mother and I are so happy; we feel very lucky to have the two of you. But this year, the world has been changing around us, and sometimes, after we put you to bed, we sit in the kitchen and say the names of cities. We say the names of countries. What would it be like to live there? Or there? Smart people should be able to make plans for their children. They should keep their children safe. So we have been talking about cities.

I've seen some very bad things this year, most of them when I was distracted. The world comes at me when I'm drinking coffee or sitting on a bus. By the time you're old enough to read this letter, the technology may be different, but right now I scroll through the news on a little handset, and so these things appear as slivers of horror in between the daily business of my life—a man burned by a phosphorus bomb as I walk to teach a class at the university, a dazed little boy about your age, pulled from the rubble of his home as I wait in line at the supermarket. Often, I don't even register them, or don't allow myself to think too hard, but sometimes they sink in further than I want them to, and I spend the rest of the day haunted by some image, some event that I didn't prepare myself to witness, another terrible truth about the world that appeared unbidden and made our family's safety and happiness feel even more precarious than before. A distraught father holds up his baby, pleading for rescue from a sinking rubber boat. Why him and not me? What would I do if we were in that situation? How would I save everyone? There are other things, horrible things that I want to protect you from for as long as possible, things that I would keep from you forever, if I could.

I don't know what will happen in the future. Maybe my worries are unfounded, but lately I've been hearing talk that sounds like it has bubbled up from the history of a time before I was born, talk about people who belong and people who don't, about real people and the others, who ought to be pushed out. The old word *cosmopolitan* has once again become a sly insult, along with a newer version, *globalist*. *Migrant*, which used to be a neutral word, is a term of abuse.

We—you, me, your mother, your sister—are migrants. That is our history. Because of that history, because of who we (and our parents) chose to love and where they chose to go, we are cosmopolitan. It's something I feel proud of, but for others, it seems to be an incitement, a rebuke.

Recently, I took a DNA test, part of a research project about migration and ancestry. It told me that some of our ancestors moved out of Africa toward central Asia. Others settled in the British Isles at the end of the last ice age. Still others drifted south, to the land between the Indus and the Ganges, and others yet encountered Neanderthals in the mountains of central Europe. Combine that with your mother's Japanese ancestry, and yet more journeys appear in your past—through the steppes of Siberia, across the South China Sea.

On your bedroom wall is an old photograph of a man with a beard. That's one of your great-great-great-grandfathers, Pandit Ajudianath Kunzru. He was from a family that had moved south from a mountain valley in Kashmir to the city of Agra on the Indian plains. Ryuichi Kitamura, the grandfather for whom you are named, was born in Osaka and made a life in a small Northern California college town. Your other grandfather, Krishna Kunzru, left Agra and went to London to work as a doctor. Your mother also moved to London, where she met me. Later, I left London for New York, where I found her again and we fell in love. You and I wouldn't be here if my father had not met my mother, a Londoner whose own father had left a tiny Welsh village and gone to study in the city.

So when people ask you where you're from, you won't

have a one-word answer for them. Some people, the kind who use *cosmopolitan* and *migrant* as insults, will call you rootless. They will call you inauthentic. They will tell you that you lack some important anchor to the earth, that your loves and attachments have less force than theirs because of all the journeys in our family's past. When they say such things, remind yourself that they, too, are migrants, even if they've forgotten it. The human story is one of continual branching movement, out of Africa to every corner of the globe. When people talk of blood and soil, as if their ancestors had sprung fully formed from the earth of a particular place, it involves a kind of forgetting. Place is not nothing, and you need to understand that many families have histories that are unlike ours. There is something noble about staying put and building, something worthy of respect. But there is also something noble about the nomad who carries a whole world in a suitcase. You were born here in New York, in the middle of a February snowstorm, and so this city will always be yours. Perhaps, if we move again to one of the other places whose names your mother and I have murmured to each other across the kitchen table, you may not grow up thinking of it as home. I'm writing to tell you that you don't need to worry about this. It's not a loss or a lack. Your experience is no more or less authentic or beautiful than a person who lives on land their ancestors have farmed for generations. It is different. You can learn from such people. And they can learn from you.

We are a family whose roots are more like aerials. We pick up signals from the air around us—ideas, affinities, tastes, coordinates. Your mother and I have made a home out of the things we love (books, above all) and done so with the help of people who have given us love. I have no power to see into the future, but I feel that we are headed into a stranger world than any I can imagine. You may live a life among nonhuman intelligences, or as part of a great assemblage of humans and machines. Of one thing I am sure— all my terms and conditions, my habits and my ways of understanding the world, are passing away. What I can do is offer my learning, such as it is, to help you on your journey, the various things I have found to be useful and true. So as you try to decide whether to build a house or a car, somewhere to stay or a vehicle in which to go, know that you make your choices as part of a tradition, that your ancestors are behind you, and that your inheritance includes love.

—New York, December 19, 2016

DREAMS FROM OUR FATHERS

Faith Adiele

Dear Dad:

As the tenth anniversary of your death approaches, I've been thinking about how I hate good-byes. January 2017 demands two of the most difficult. We must take our arms from around the first black family to occupy the White House, in the same gesture letting go of our civil rights dream, the bloody, centuries-long battle that birthed both Obama and me. He was Hope, as I am Faith, both of us Halfrican—civil rights babies born of optimistic white American mothers and black African fathers.

Optimistic, because even though the year of Obama's birth Herbert Lee, a black farmer with nine children, was shot in the head for trying to register black voters, it was also the year the Freedom Rides rocked the South and established a generation of youth leaders. Optimistic, because even though the year of my birth the Klan bombed four little black girls in a Birmingham church and Medgar Evers and President Kennedy were gunned down, it was also the year that established our road map for today—America's dispossessed marching on Washington in unprecedented numbers to demand freedom and articulate our dream.

Eight Novembers ago, I sat stunned amid rejoicing campaign volunteers, Dad, wishing you'd lasted long enough to witness it for yourself. "I can't believe it," I whispered. "We did it. I can't believe it. Yes, we *can*." We, the literal embodiment of our nation's struggle, white against black, haves versus have-nots, would not only show how to come together but also lead the way. I was less surprised this past November. "No, you can't," the Demagogue Narcissist railed. "Only I can!" And so, the dream died.

Dad, it's also the tenth anniversary of your Homegoing, which, if I were a better daughter to your imperfect father, I'd be flying to Nigeria to mark with all the dizzying ritual and money hemorrhaging due someone of your political stature and personal sacrifice. But instead of buying goats and hiring abattoirs, I trudge through America, too heavy of heart to bid farewell to Obama or you. If I could drag myself to the village to stand at your rust-red grave, what could I possibly say?

Our family has always communicated better via the page. That's where we first met, after all. You wooed first my mother and then me through letters—sheaf after sheaf of white onionskin and cornflower-blue airmail smeared with spidery fountain pen ink, pulsating with possibility. You appeared at age twenty-nine, a grad student at Washington State University, educating yourself for the promise of independence. She was a seventeen-year-old freshwoman obsessed with geopolitics, the daughter of Nordic immigrants who transferred her to a university on the other side of the state to separate you. Instead, you wrote every day: *Well, Jo, I don't know what the future holds but quote me as saying, "By 1971 I will be in the heart of Nigerian politics." Possibly that public servant that is called Minister of Foreign Affairs (here you call him Secretary of State). But don't curse and swear at me yet as "politicking."*

We shan't. After all, Nigeria had just regained its independence from Britain a few weeks after your arrival in Washington. In a decade spent schooling abroad, first in London and then the USA (lured away from the colonial master by news of black civil rights), you'd never been home, never seen independent Nigeria, never been free. Who wouldn't be ambitious? *I think that the individual cannot exist in a vacuum. Cannot exist in isolation. He is the member of a tribe, a church, a family, a political party or a social club. He is influenced by these things and does himself influence them. We don't live for ourselves. We live for others. Perhaps in the African scale of values, freedom ranks quite high. I would say that perhaps the best role any group ought to play is that of freedom.* And though we didn't meet until I was nearly the age you were then, I knew, just as Obama knew and Trump does not, what was expected of us in the New World. Freedom had been too hard won for our family of Finnish indentured servants and Swedish laborers and American single mothers and colonized Africans. *We don't live for ourselves.*

So when they called, you answered. *I want you to know that this is not a good-bye,* you declared naïvely from an ocean liner in the middle of the Atlantic. *I shall look forward to our meeting so long as we are all alive.* The ship docked in Lagos four months before my second birthday, and you dashed down the gangplank into election madness. The Brits, architects of that messy creation called Nigeria (and now of Brexit), set you up for failure, handing over power to the north. Now the new nation—northern desert / southern tropics, northern Muslim / southern Christian, northern Hausaland / western Yorubaland / eastern Igboland—chafed. *The pace is quick, upsetting and dangerous, as each political party and its supporters are hard put to big fights.* You worried: *One gets the impression that something is boiling and will soon boil over!*

Back here, we were fighting for the same things. Voting rights activists prepared to march from Selma to Montgomery. On Bloody Sunday, two days before my second birthday, Alabama state troopers attacked six hundred peaceful demonstrators with billy clubs, tear gas, and bullwhips. Today, Republicans exchange billy clubs for legislation chipping away at the Voting Rights Act; corporations tear gas us with ads and reality television until the only vote we care about is *American Idol*; but police departments stick with the tried and true, slaughtering black men in the streets, on camera if need be.

Into Nigeria's stew pot you leaped, giddy from the lengthy sea voyage and "excessive heat" on your slim, dark suit: *Things have so changed that I am not sure of anything nor anybody's whereabouts!* You were thirty-two, and it was your first time in a black-owned country. *Nigeria is indeed a new place! You have no conception of the degree of change and conflict.* Neither did you. Something is always boiling. Someone always wants to play the colonial master. It didn't take long for Nigeria to get caught up in us/them rhetoric, for your leaders to start playing the ethnic division card and inciting citizens to turn against their countrymen and neighbors for supposedly stealing their jobs and their good luck. Demagoguery: the fastest way up for a politician. Does any of this sound familiar?

It was inconceivable to you at the time, in Africa's greatest, wealthiest, best-educated nation, the world's fourth-largest democracy. But if a racist, misogynist billionaire who made his fortune bilking workers can put on a baseball cap, perform as working-class, and seize control of the so-called Standard of Democracy, then certainly a few Nigerian soldiers and politicians can go on the airwaves and whip up a frenzy. Did you see the warning signs like I see them now? Were you saying, *Things like that don't happen here*, as the pogroms started? As thirty thousand of your Igbo brothers were killed and fifty thousand wounded or maimed? As those attempting to flee the north were rounded up at airports and bus and railway stations and mutilated, raped, killed by soldiers and civilians, the corpses then sent home to Igboland?

During the main phase of the killings, only fifty years ago, you wrote to us: *Oh, you wouldn't believe it that my senior sister is one of the people who were killed. She was visiting some relations in the North. It is hard to believe but ours could be any day now. The country I love so much is in flames but I hope it will survive!* Your last letter was written before Christmas: *I find it extremely uncomfortable to narrate my story regarding the mass killing of Easterners in Northern Nigeria. I lost a score of relatives there. The unrest is still with us. Nigeria is facing the worst crisis in its history and if we escape a complete disintegration, we are lucky indeed. We live in fear every day.* Dad, what would you say to me today, uncomfortable or not, now that the unrest is with us? Now that we live in fear—though to be fair, most of Black America has always lived this way and doesn't have the luxury of bemoaning this one. *You remember that I used to have eight sisters and one brother. Two of my sisters plus my mother plus my father are all dead.*

You were happy when the east seceded, forming the Republic of Biafra. It felt like self-determination, this first challenge to colonial borders. But a few months later, just after the U.S. Supreme Court legalized interracial marriage in *Loving v. Virginia*, Nigeria declared war and invaded. Your letters stopped. All we saw were the horrific, iconic images of starving Biafran children my age and the horrific, iconic images of Martin and Senator Bobby Kennedy gunned down. I wish I could ask what kept you going during those years of war and silence. How to live when your own government wants you dead.

Finally, nine months after the end of the war, your letter arrived at the family farm. Battered, crosshatched with different-colored inks, it bore only our names and the town: *Sunnyside, Washington*. The trail of inks revealed that it had slowly crept through the streets of Washington, D.C. (where thirty-nine years later your daughter would wave a YES WE CAN banner at the inauguration), until the postmaster declared *No such street as Sunnyside* and forwarded it west to Washington State.

And suddenly, after three years of silence, there you were, claiming to have lost hope but sounding optimistic as ever: *Warmest Greetings. I have been wondering how I can reach you to let you know that I am still alive. I survived the Nigerian civil war although I lost everything including my diary which contained your address. Our home, assets, proper-*

ties, my library and all my books, certificates and diplomas, thesis, my Ph.D. dissertation, my academic gown and hood and everything you can imagine were destroyed. All I now have is the outfit I was wearing on the day the war ended. I look forward to hearing from you having lost every hope of seeing you again.

Whenever I'm feeling whiny or weak, I read you. You who forgave your fellow Nigerians, because a national narrative was more important to you than a victim narrative. *Conditions are far from normal here. I still lack more than 90 percent of the essentials. Money is in extreme short supply and my monthly pay can hardly sustain the many dependents I have acquired as a result of the civil war for a week! The devastation is so overwhelming that whatever is being done is only a drop in a limitless ocean! We lost quite a number of our "clan" to air-raids, bullets and shelling! It is quite a torture to remember them and I would rather let the sleeping dogs lie. I find it quite unbearable to have to recall the tragedies and wouldn't be doing Faith any good sending a catalogue of dead relatives! When she is older it will become part of the history she will have to piece together, I suppose.* As the vanquished, your options were few. Still, after three years of devastating resistance, you chose to stay. To rebuild. To make Nigeria great, which to the visionary means inclusive and new.

Eight Januarys ago, I packed my Nigerian brocades and head ties and drove to Washington, D.C., to attend Our (as we would say in Nigeria) Inauguration. At every truck stop and gas station in Red-State-Land and Blue-State-Land, black folks grinned giddily at one another. It took so much to get Obama there that everyone wanted to celebrate, with parties all over the District, every one of my kin—writers, artists, and activists—lining up to perform.

Ten Januarys ago, I returned to Nigeria for Our Burial. It took so much to say good-bye to you: 1 archbishop, 4 bishops, 1 choir dressed in outfits with your face on them, 1 eze (local king), 3 rainmen, 3 cows, dozens of goats, hundreds of yams, 60 cords of wood, 2,000 portions of rice, a cooling van of drinks, a private army for hire, 6 weeks' preparation, 1,600 T-shirts, 1,600 fans, 1,600 calendars, 2 costume changes, and a band. As eldest daughter, I sat up front in the hearse, a portrait of you in my lap, villagers rushing into the street to witness your return home. Inside the compound gates, young men in white suits with black T-shirts, wraparound sunglasses, and white gloves danced around the courtyard, your casket atop their shoulders, lowering themselves down-down-down, until practically on their knees, then up-up-up, shoulders shrugging, no hands, hardly weighed down by your now-tiny body.

But in memory you are huge: *I am a new generation of Africans. We believe in the future role of that continent. We are convinced it has a destiny and a contribution to make to the world community. It has long languished, slept, misunderstood, exploited, pushed around, and spoken for. Now it is Africa's hour to do and speak to the world.* In his eulogy, the archbishop extolled your good works as commissioner of education, mentioned adopted children from West to South Africa. *We don't live for ourselves.* My eulogy was culled from admirers in Nigeria and America who called you "one of the few honest politicians" and "a giant not afraid to sacrifice for his country." *In the African scale of values, freedom ranks quite high.*

So many African leaders since you have continued the colonial project—devolving into megalomaniacal dictators with no respect for the press or voting rights, distracting with ethnic tensions while handing keys to cronies and sticky-fingered offspring. And they're not alone, it seems. Trevor Noah, biracial South African brother to East African Obama and West African me, quips, "Zuma and Trump [are] like brothers from another mother!" Dad, your heart was already breaking to see Africa's leaders; what would you make of this anti-intellectual running the country that educated you? What did you learn that can save us now?

Chief Odumegwu Ojukwu, the son of a millionaire, our former leader who personally financed the Biafran struggle against the Nigerian government's attacks, famously wrote: *We are humans. We live. We fight, because the decision to be free is a decision taken freely and collectively.* So, when he called, you answered: *A free, united, forward-looking, self-respecting Africa needs dedicated, clear-seeing, committed and self-emancipated citizens who have the guts to identify and live with the aspirations, yearnings, problems and promises of emerging peoples. In this fight for reality and right, I cannot see myself taking a dubious part or staying on the side of the ring. I must and will step inside. I will take the right stand. I will not be neutral.*

Dad, on this, the tenth anniversary of your Homegoing, perhaps I can be a better daughter not by flying there to honor your political stature and personal sacrifice but by staying here and taking your words to heart. To embody you, I choose the Nation over Faith. Choose the Fight over love. No, the fight as love.

AMERICA

Parnaz Foroutan

Here at our sea-washed, sunset gates shall stand
A mighty woman with a torch, whose flame
Is the imprisoned lightning, and her name
Mother of Exiles. From her beacon-hand
Glows world-wide welcome; her mild eyes command
The air-bridged harbor that twin cities frame.
"Keep ancient lands, your storied pomp!" cries she
With silent lips. "Give me your tired, your poor,
Your huddled masses yearning to breathe free,
The wretched refuse of your teeming shore.
Send these, the homeless, tempest-tost to me,
I lift my lamp beside the golden door!

> —Emma Lazarus, excerpt from "The New Colossus,"
> inscribed on the pedestal of the Statue of Liberty

For my mother, that night so many years ago, when she walked that desolate highway, with a baby in her arms, and me, a small child, tired, trudging beside her,

Behind you was the war in Iran. Behind you were air raid sirens that pierced the black of the night. The whistles of bombs, the shattering of bones, the rubble in daylight that no one wanted to believe. Behind you the dark Sisters of Islam, wrapped in their cloaks of death, the painted portraits of martyrs on buildings.

"Young boys," you whispered to your friends. "They give young boys plastic keys and tell them that it is their entry into heaven, then send them into battle."

Behind you, men who felt nothing but greed and greed and greed. Saddam with his missiles newly gifted by the United States, the ayatollah across from him, with his missiles secretly purchased from the United States, and between them, the young boys promised heaven, clutching their plastic keys.

I came home from school and told you, "We can't listen to music anymore, Mama. The teacher said. She said if my parents listen to music to tell her."

I came home from school and told you, "The teacher told us that we have to wear the hijab, at the park, in the streets, at the market. She said if we saw one of our classmates not wearing the veil to tell her."

You looked at my father. And that was all I understood. A look followed by silence. Among the adults, a silence. And fear.

One afternoon, you came to pick me up after school, but the school was silent. We weren't on the playground, running, playing, chattering. The janitor told you and the rest of the worried mothers that the teachers had taken their students for a walk, to the nearby cemetery, to place flowers on the graves of the martyred.

You responded with silence. Because those who spoke disappeared.

We went to bed waiting to be awoken by the wail of sirens. I remember. My father running through dark hallways, my infant sister and me in his arms, running down dark staircases, to the basement where the other families sat huddled, waiting. We listened to the planes flying overhead, while the landlord muffled with his large hand his wife's endless scream.

In the mornings, in the classrooms, they'd tell your young daughter to cloak herself with shame. To report, to her teacher, who'd report, in turn, to the State, if there was joy in your home, or laughter.

That night, on that long highway, you walked away from this story. It was a story you had to leave behind. Because you couldn't allow your daughters to tremble in dark basements, to wait and pray that the plane would pass overhead. You didn't want them to see the mangled buildings, the broken mothers, the painted martyrs.

And the unthinkable, that one of those planes passing overhead might just target the beds your children slept in.

You carried your infant daughter in one arm, and walked with me, a child six years of age, tired, trudging beside you. You left that nightmare behind.

And you left behind other things, too. The elm trees that lined your street. The familiar scent of autumn. The baker's smile when he handed you the fresh bread, the song of the peddlers in the street, the sound of strangers around you talking, haggling, buying, singing, speaking, fighting in a language you understood. Your friends. Your career. Your home. Your dreams. Your family. Your memories. Pots, pans, the fine silver spoons and forks. Photographs. Heirlooms. Your favorite dresses. Your father's grave. The colorful wares of the markets at the new year. Streets you knew by name. Cab drivers who recited poetry. The halls of your old university. You left whatever you couldn't fit into a single suitcase behind you and closed the door of your home for the last time, the dishes washed, the beds made, the curtains drawn, thinking, *Perhaps, perhaps we will come back*, and you shut the door, and left, without knowing if you'd ever find home again.

This letter is for you, Mother. On that night, on that long and endless highway, with all your stories left behind you, as you walked in the direction of America.

This letter is for all mothers who choose exile, who walk away from everything they know in search of a safe haven.

Who carry their tired children upon their backs through deserts, with home left behind them, and the hope of America at the end of that long, perilous journey.

For the mothers who help their frightened children into crowded boats that sail into the tempest-tossed seas. For the mothers who ignore their own hunger so that they can feed their children until they reach the plenty they dream of giving. This letter is for the mothers who shield the bodies of their sleeping babes through the dark nights while planes fly overhead, mothers who pray of giving their children a home where they might sleep safely.

America is yours.

She always has been. America is the Mother of Exiles. That is her given name, and it is from this dream of mothers that she was conceived. She is the end to that perilous road, the safe shore of that stormy ocean, the refuge from the darkness, the terror, the suffering. She is the plenty, the giver, the one who holds the torch, the flame of which is the imprisoned lightning that will guide us home.

Pay no heed to the darkness, the open mouth of greed, the hateful speech, the walls and the guns and the men who bare their teeth at her golden doors. America is yours. Your prayers conceived her, your dreams for your children brought her into being, and your children make her what she is meant to be. They build her. Fashion her bones, sturdy her structures, make her beautiful and strong. America belongs to you, to all mothers who dream of her.

So light the small flame of your heart, cup your hands around it to protect it from the savage and the storm, and walk forth into that darkness, because I tell you, that flame, that bit of light you carry, that flickering hope, that has the power to illuminate even the blackest of nights. Hold steady, walk forth, and burn with truth, with love, with compassion, burn brightly because soon, the dawn will come.

To my mother, on that highway, on that endless night, when she walked toward the glow of that torch, with lightning imprisoned in her heart.

To all the mothers who've walked toward this light,

Welcome.
Home.

DEAR CHEBON

Chip Livingston

Chipper Boy,

I don't expect this to frighten you none, Chebon, receiving my message like this, as you've always been tuned for reception. But write it down, so you remember, and share my words with those who might need them. I'm taking advantage of the holiday prayers and chimney smoke to work a bit of your paw-paw's old Solstice magic to make sure this missive gets through. Obviously, you'll have to clean up my grammar some. I could do all sorts of things with a wrench or hammer, but words, Grandson, those are your tools. I took just enough book learning to sign my name away on bills and send you short notes in college.

Away is a funny word to think about, here from the spirit world you might call West of Heaven, but we're closer than most people think. Your ancestors aren't just floating around in some far-off place. We're also there on the earth, watching with you as the creeks freeze and thaw, smiling and laughing mostly at your forgetfulness, reminded of our own fleshly shortcomings. But where we are, we know a wholer sense of empathy. Especially now, Grandson, when you're holding on to worries larger than your heads conceive the world to be.

You forget, Chebon, some of the things I told you as we walked the land, picking up empty beer cans and gathering pecans. The trash we can recycle, and the task to break the stubborn shells is worth the sweet inside. But just now, you ain't worrying none about pecans or the forty cents a pound we got for bags of aluminum. You think the whole world is ending. But only parts of it are ending—and only as you've known them, the little what you know of it. We keep learning.

The United States has always been a figment of some white folks' imagination. Democracy? Tell your paw-paw a better one. You took some history from me and some from books, but what you seem to forget is that what you stand on stays forever. That land in Alabama, Colorado, Uruguay, and all the rest of it, it's been here since crawfish brought the mud up and long before the thought of humans. That land will be here long after the memory of us, Chebon. The earth is taking a beating, sure, and tides will rise. But the land itself withstands. As do we, son, but in forms you don't yet understand but will in time to come.

Time to come, Grandson, you'll also understand this election as a duration all people face and our people in particular have already several times survived. Your blood's a testament to that long line of troubling history; it's nothing you can't handle. The president-elect of the United States in the year 2017 is not going to be what ends human life. Don't believe apocalyptic lies. There is no Armageddon. But, of course, there will be consequences.

Confusion, pain, division. Fear. It won't always be clear who or what to believe. You sure won't have to dig up distractions. They'll be near. But so will the gathering of a new kind of nation. The continent is calling out for its true citizens, restoring the balance of brown people who first emerged upon its mud; it's telling you the land is almost ready for your occupation. You're coming out from underground—just like your ancestors. Your volume now is just an ankle rattle, but it's growing toward a hum. Listen for the drums that lead toward syncopation. Syncopation! How's that for your paw-paw's eighth-grade education! But it's true, Chebon. Trust me. There's a song if you listen. That's a promise. Keep listening until you know the tune. Then write a new verse. Sing that prayer into the world. Direct the chorus.

Chipper Boy, this ain't a scolding. Sure, I'm prone to coaching, but this is also a celebration. You exist. Despite everything they've done to us, you exist. With everything they're doing now to silence and undermine your objections and confidence, Chebon, you exist. As long as you're alive to witness and protest, you still exist. So don't get down. Instead, get up and shout. Then dance. Don't forget to stomp and dance. Feel your feet on the sand. That's your freedom.

Remember the balance and share as much good news as you acknowledge the bad. Spread even more good news. This trouble too shall pass. And what comes after this muddy patch is so much better, more solid, more united in humanity than the planet has yet seen in our living history.

This message is a recognition of you and the Helpers who clamor at the real chaos of earth's growing pains. It's an awakening. A celebration of a new awareness. And it's a great big thank-you. We're grateful, son—*Mvto, Chebon*—to everyone who's paying attention. We're paying attention. All Creation is listening. Make your noise, but also remember to quiet down and distinguish the truth from illusion. Keep your chin up. You're not going back underground, but there are times you'll have to tread water. This is just another one of them. And you know how to swim.

But the earth will remain. And we're not going any-where. Remember as you walk the land your relatives pre-pared for you: Prepare the world as best you can for seven generations. Life is still a celebration. Trust me, Grandson. There's a reason we don't have a word for *good-bye*.

Your Paw-Paw

Branches

HUMAN RIGHTS IS THE HANDHOLD, PASS IT ON

Mohja Kahf

Dear Fayza,

Understandable to feel sad and scared because the country has elected Trump. I hear you, habibti.

It might help to see from a perspective of decades. Decades before, decades after. Think like a tree. This is one ring, and a tree trunk will have many. This might be just a thin one. Think like a tree, and send those roots down deep digging for water through whatever soil. You will look back on this from better moments, decades hence.

So that may help us to detach a bit from the outcome. Not "detach" as in "not care"! Act with hope, but detach from hope for a specific outcome. Because we don't know how this story goes on. Many things may happen yet. Buffalo herds may appear. Eagles may fly in. And they may not, but you keep trudging on because your actions may help other helpful actions to unfold, and then who knows. We don't know what else might happen along the way. Just don't expect; don't get too attached to one expectation. Keep a Plan B and a Plan C, and diversify your survival tool kit.

Meanwhile, there is struggle. There is no ending to it; it's ongoing. Struggle for human rights is not about one man or woman at the top; it requires constant work. We knew we were going to have to keep on with that anyway, because the injustice is systemic and is spread throughout the order that exists. You who came of age in the past decade have had eight years of a Black U.S. president, and that gloss looked good, and there were even a few inches gained on some issues such as health care, and maybe that can cause a person to relax a bit. But think of how exponentially drone attacks increased under Obama, how many Black people were shot by police under Obama, because the violence is systemic. How many of the people now hearteningly pledging to sign up for a Muslim registry signed up for Black Lives Matter or protested the discriminatory immigration program NSEERS? The National Security Entry-Exit Registration System subjected my students from the Middle East to hours of interrogation and intimidation every time they reentered after going home to visit their families, arbitrarily barred tons of innocent people from entry, and was ineffective against terrorism anyway. It's systemic injustice we are after changing, and we should not ever be lulled.

Remember this: any legal gains that were made through the human rights struggle over the past decades are not going to drain away overnight. They're law now. My town's civil rights ordinance saying LGBTQ people have the same rights as everyone else is law as of last year, and Trump being president doesn't change that law in my town. No one person being in office can easily cause those gains to vanish—but we have to stay on it. We will have to fight any effort to roll them back every step of the way, in grassroots organizing and in courts. But they were not just changes made because of one man or one party at the top; whole coalitions of people were involved. Those coalitions are not going to dissolve overnight. Those people are still here. People power is renewable energy.

As a child, I lived in a small midwestern town so racist I felt suicidal. I thought it was me. I thought I was just not what they used to call in my school a "good citizen," that must be why the teachers looked at me with such skepticism or did not see me, or gave me a "demerit point" when they did see me. Every morning in junior high, I had to pass a gauntlet of boys leaning against the wall, calling me every filthy name they could think of, epithets related to the fact that I was a foreigner in their midst, had a different religion, and dressed differently (it wasn't even just the hijab thing— on top of everything, I often wore these home-sewn pants hiked up to my chin—you don't want to know). This happened right in the front school lobby, but no one in authority ever noticed or stopped it. And some of the teachers were undoubtedly Klan, and yet even they, along with most of the rest, were probably "nice" people. If you met them and you were one of them, you'd experience them as such nice people—that's how I knew it was my fault, my rotten character.

As an adult, I learned how to identify exactly what people in that school and that town were doing and not doing. I now know what terms such as *gaslighting* mean, concepts you have from the get-go. I gained, from having gone through it, the resources my parents didn't have so I can help my children not to have this kind of experience, even if systemic racism is still there. You and I both know how to identify it now, and we have allies who help us with that. (Also, I try not to make my kids wear home-sewn pants. Got the class privilege now to finagle that.) You have the concepts to save yourself from going under to things that can drag you into self-blame and suicidal depression stemming from being in a crazy-making racist setup. And you have me to remind you, if you forget. And here's one reminder: avoid filling your life with "nice" people who find racism invisible or who second-guess your every instinct on it while indulging in liberal hand-wringing, because eventually, this will drain your inner resources. Seek out people who are "woke"—tell me if I just used a hip word correctly?

If, in reacting to this election, we old fogies bring up the decades of racism, xenophobia, and sexism we have experienced in this country, it's not to tell young folks not to worry because we've been through it before. It's not to diminish the bizarreness of this election or the seriousness of the dangers ahead, or to be optimistic or unrealistic. It's not to idly reminisce, and it's not to strike the victim pose. It's to call to mind the inner resources we developed to fight racism and xenophobia, and to call to mind the strategies that produced little bits of success along the way, and to remember that we're stronger now for having fought this fight before. And it sucks that your generation, instead of being able to give your energies to other issues, has to fight this anew, but it's not really new. We say that it's not new to remind you that you have those inner and outer strengths with you. You have them inside you, and you have them accumulated from previous generations. We survived it before with what felt like fewer resources, and look at all the resources you—we—have for surviving it now. You amaze me with your cutting-edge tools for this work, your inter-sectional concepts, and your insta-snappa-whatcha ways of organizing. Your vision goes far beyond what I ever had at your age and takes my breath away. You can do this. Heave to. We can do this.

It all starts with Black people, whatever we have learned about the civil rights struggle in this country. It starts with Indigenous peoples. Check in with them, and witness against our own anti-Blackness in our own immigrant and Muslim American communities and our own ignorance of Indigenous struggles. The Quran says to stand firmly as witnesses for justice, "even against yourselves, or your parents, or your kin, and rich or poor" (4:135). We cannot just expect to hop on and benefit from the wisdom they gained in their struggles if we do not also hold ourselves account-able for participating in degrees of white colonial privilege. And how about our community buying into snotty middle-class oppression toward the poor and the working class, can we get good against that? American Jews are targets of this newly emboldened racism, too, and despite the fact that the Zionism held by many Jewish Americans is racist against us as Arabs, we stand with them against anti-Semitism while still demanding Zionist accountability for massacring Palestinian rights. Human rights are the axis, from here to my Syria, from here to your Palestine. "Let not the hatred of any people against you swerve you from dealing justly" (Quran 5:8). Striving for equal human rights, clear across the globe, is the only firm handhold that can pull all of us through all of this.

Try out this idea: maybe it is useful that the racism is now out in the open. It never stopped being there systemically, but now the cover is blown, and it's naked. This allows people to demand accountability and to make choices. A young brown boy in a mostly white middle school in this country, a boy I love, told me last year, "Dude, racism was a long time ago. Now Obama's president!" It was a challenge to try to show him how racism is still present and actually endangers his own life, knowledge I believe that he needs for survival every time he crosses the street in front of a cop car. Young people just coming up now will be more clear-eyed that they do need to mobilize against racism; it's not just a lesson in their social studies class. One last thing: less than half the voting population voted. And just under half of that number voted Trump; as you know, the popular vote was for the not-openly-racist candidate. That means, hey, really only about a fourth of the country hates us and/ or hates Black people, LGBTQ folk, Latinx peoples, Indigenous peoples, and immigrants. And we already knew that, right?

Call me if you need to talk. I got you, habibti.

Hugs,
Mohja

PS: Buy emergency contraception now, just in case. You're too young to remember how long the morning-after pill took to get on the market in the United States, and who knows if it might soon be hard to get again. Also, make sure your passport is in working order. Check in with allies often, and have their phone numbers on you—and not just on your cell phone. And check in with whoever you know who might need the same kind of help from you. Pass it on!

YOU

Achy Obejas

You

You are standing on a wild horizon, bleak and blurry, at the beginning of what seems, even in its adolescence, a cursed and forsaken century: incapable of memory, bombarded by apocryphal stories and promises that—even as they're pronounced, even as they fall from our leaders' mouths like white spinels and moissanites—betray their false sparkle.

You, you

You're confounded by leaders as authentic as Princess Caraboo and the scrap metal Lustig sold as the Eiffel Tower. Oh, how they chant their chants: *War is peace, freedom is slavery*—and most importantly—*ignorance is strength*. That's right: The less you know, the more indignant. The less you know, the more protected. The less you know, the more correct you're bound to be. The chorus is no less than: *Say it loud, I'm here and I'm proud.* Doesn't that sound familiar? Take a breath. Let the chorus go silent, walk away on a path of your own design and determination, even if you lose your way a few times during the journey. Don't be afraid of the loneliness.

You, you, you

You must have a brutal clarity about the river of tears that brought us here, to you, and how that river flooded Al-Andalus, Jamestown, Ulster, Yangzhou, Salem, Lancaster, Warsaw, Constantinople, Port-au-Prince, Boston, Sand Creek, Gippsland, Frog Lake, Wounded Knee, the Armenian Highlands, Guaymas, Jeju Island, Istanbul, Berlin, Cabinda, Chicago, Ponce, Katyn, Odessa, Kefalonia, Manila, Haifa, Lydda, Hula, Batang Kali, No Gun Ri, Nairobi, Sharpeville, Paris, Jacinto Vera, Zanzibar, Hue, My Lai and My Khe, Leopoldville, Mexico City, Borgå, Karen, Delhi, Choeung Ek, Buganda, Tochni, San Salvador, Derry, Munich, Ezeiza, Marichjhapi, Gwangju, Palmyra, El Mozote, Hama, Lucanamarca, Dujail, Clifton Hills, Belfast, Tiananmen Square, Aramoana, Barrios Altos, Waco, Sivas, Cape Town, Kigali, the West Bank, Sarajevo, Luxor, East Timor, Port Arthur, Acteal, Omagh, Andijan, Haditha, Blacksburg, Kabul, Kandahar, Abu Ghraib, Charleston, Lafayette, Orlando, Darfur, Aleppo, and how we drank that river water, and how that river poisoned our blood, and how that blood became the instrument with which we write the history we bequeath to you.

You, you, you, you

You may take pride in the lattice of scars your ancestors received from the lash and for how long your blood pumped underwater while they waited for you to bob to the surface just so they could drown you again, and how long you kept your eyes open when your head rolled, and how long you sang aloud while your limbs burned . . . but hold on to the truth of how sometimes your people held the lash, and sometimes you knotted the witch's wrist, and sometimes loosed the guillotine and threw the match. Because none of us is truly free of past misdeeds, and that will help you forgive in the future.

You, you, you, you, you

You must not take anyone's word for anything. Remember that trust cannot grow from lies and contempt, that the only thing those engender is capitulation to an unacceptably false reality. Be wary—be kind, yes, but be wary. Ask questions. Is this real? Is this really real? Seek out the answers—the many different and conflicting answers. Insist on them. Weigh them. Reflect. Be a witness. Take what you learn, prick your finger, and write a new story.

You, you, you, you, you, you

You must learn to have a sharp eye, a steady step, an arm that's strong enough to carry more than just you, a heart that loves hard and true, and a sense of timing that's as precise as the most precise atomic clock or the moon. Commit. Be a witness. Take what you learn, prick your finger, and write a new story to be read in the days to come. Then listen: listen to the stories others have written and that are read aloud like a song.

You, you, you, you, you, you, you

Know that you will fail, and fail royally, over and over again. And that each failure must be executed with dignity because each failure is also an inspiration, a demonstration of the system's weakness, a nod to the possibilities, a lesson to all who testify and a call to reflect and decipher the moment of failure, the weak spot, in order to reinforce it or get around it or otherwise reign over it so the failure can become something else next time, whether you're here to see it or not. Commit. Be a witness. Take what you learn, prick your finger, and write it down so it can be read as testimony in the days to come. Then read all the proclamations that are entrusted to you, bind them, encrypt them, discuss them, repeat them to everyone you meet.

You, you, you, you, you, you, you, you

You must learn to live with your pain, which means wearing it like a medal but also, and perhaps mostly, giving in to its limitations, to its call for refuge and balm, sometimes with others, sometimes alone. And in that pain, you must find the formula to understand the pain of others and be their refuge and balm, if they let you, if they want you, and to be that without expecting payback or reward. Commit. Be a witness. Prick your finger and offer it to your companions in battle.

You, you, you, you, you, you, you, you, you

As a last resort, you may try the fog test. Breathe and see what happens, see if your heat makes them sweat, or, if they step right up to kiss you back, with clear and honest intent.

You, you, you, you, you, you, you, you, you, you

You must accept that you cannot go it alone. That the future that must be rescued is a world upon a world, ours, mine, upon yours and the next generation's, an endless horizon. Lock your bleeding fingers with one another. Listen attentively: how, amid the chaos and uproar, our commitment to each other, to the stories we tell and the battles we fight together, there's a stirring of hope like a fluttering of pages, of wings.

A TIME TO DEMAND THE IMPOSSIBLE

Viet Thanh Nguyen

To my fellow writers and artists; to my fellow readers and lovers of art; to my fellow believers in peace and a more perfect world:

For many of us, perhaps almost all of us, the feeling is that we are in a time of crisis. Donald Trump triumphed, an accomplishment that many, except his most ardent supporters, deemed to be impossible. For all of his faults, and they are many, he made a daring bet that paid off. He told a story that half of America wanted to hear. Hillary Clinton and the Democrats, in contrast, played defense. They went to the center and said to the left, "Take it or leave it." They yearned for the possible. This is the sad, pallid vision of American liberals, and perhaps for too many writers and artists as well.

Now that playing it safe as a strategic and moral principle has failed, can we try something different? Can we refuse to reconcile with Republicans, who stood their ground and got what their base wanted? The Democrats don't seem to understand the principle of negotiation, which is to begin from what you want, not what you will settle for. Faced with an Obama Supreme Court nominee, the Republicans refused to budge, and now they will get their pick and define everyone's future. The Republicans may have the wrong principles, but at least they have principles and stand by them.

Here's what I have to say to American liberals and leftists: instead of listening to the strategists, who don't believe it's possible to dramatically change our society, can we finally be bold and listen to the artists and the outsiders and the radicals and the freaks and the avant-garde and the base and the youth and the anarchists and all those who don't want to do business as usual with the limousine liberalism of both the elite Democrats and Republicans? Can we listen to the dreamers instead of the doubters? Can we dare to demand the impossible?

Here's what I want, in the 1992 words of the artist Zoe Leonard: "I want a dyke for president. I want a person with AIDS for president and I want a fag for vice president and I want someone with no health insurance and I want someone who grew up in a place where the earth is so saturated with toxic waste that they didn't have a choice about getting leukemia." Her powerful and provocative text goes on for thirty-four lines in this manner. "I want a Black woman for president," she writes, and if you say that's preposterous, you evidently did not see that the preposterous happened with the victory of Donald Trump.

Leonard speaks about the marginal, the forgotten, the exploited, the abused, the impoverished, and the persecuted. She draws no distinction in terms of race, for one could easily be white and rural and fall into one of these categories as one could be minority and urban. This is the dream of solidarity and coalition among the down-and-out that the leadership of the Democratic Party has abandoned, favoring instead a chummy cosmopolitanism with the globe-trotting financial brokers whose ultimate allegiance is to capitalism, not to country. The white majority has chosen white identity politics and rejected this, but our response should not be more anemic liberalism or our own version of a limited identity politics.

Of course, the Democratic Party supports the civil and social rights of the down-and-out, which is important, but it won't support in any meaningful way the one strategy that might provide economic uplift: redistribution. *Redistribution* is a more fearsome *R* word than *rights*, and fear of redistribution (whether it be of income or of opportunities) unifies the leadership of the two parties. But here's an even more fearsome *R* word: *revolution*.

Trump has led a revolution, but it will not be the kind that leads to a more just society. The version he offers is the strongman's revolution, executed from the top in the name of those on the bottom. Even as they are entertained by the spectacle of a shoot-from-the-hip president and by the scapegoating of undocumented immigrants, even as they yawn at the videos of black people shot dead, they will not likely see genuine economic change, for it is doubtful that a strongman can or will create more and better jobs for them. A strong man, by definition, respects other strong men, not the weakness of the masses or of women.

An actual revolution might be a real possibility if the United States cannot create more and better jobs. Because what will the future hold when almost all the profits of capitalism go to the 1 percent, and some of the profits go to the next 10 percent, and almost none go to the rest? How does capitalism sustain itself when more and more of the people cannot afford to buy the things that capitalism offers because they are no longer needed to make those things? That's the basic contradiction of our new übercapitalism, a model that somehow thinks it can make a profit by providing services while eliminating workers.

A model that combines rights and redistribution can save capitalism from its own contradiction, but capitalists cannot be trusted to save themselves. This includes not just Donald Trump but also Hillary Clinton. As Slavoj Žižek says of liberals, "What they are really afraid of is actual radical social change." A better story than what Trump or Clinton offered America is needed. It can't come from the compromised, cynical insiders, as our president-elect saw. Often, the outsiders see us better than we on the inside can see ourselves. Artists and writers are usually among these outsiders, but even so, our art and writing are often not that radical, or even very political.

It's time for us to get political as we once did in great numbers in the 1930s, the period of the "Old Left" that reached its culmination with the "New Left" of the 1960s. The forces of progressive change in the United States developed in parallel with the movements for decolonization worldwide. But since the 1960s, the right wing has pushed back, domestically and globally. Those who exploit fear and believe in walls and borders are on the ascent. The dreams of liberation seem to be fading before the aggressive spirit of ethnic and national segregation.

Those of us who would tear down walls and eradicate borders, and who believe in both inclusion and equality, need to use our talents to help build a coalition of left and right, black and white, and everything in between, just large enough to move the country—and hopefully the world—in a more inclusive, equitable, and just direction. Is this unrealistic? As Ursula K. Le Guin said, writers need to be "realists of a larger reality." While the right wing has think tanks to develop and promulgate its vision, the left has most of the writers and the artists. Now those writers and artists need to recognize that their art has an important role to play in transforming our world. Now is the time for a commitment to an art that is explicitly political.

Leonard was prophetic about our current situation in 1992, although perhaps she was simply willing to say what has been evident for a long time to anyone with principles: "I want to know why we started learning somewhere down the line that a president is always a clown: always a john and never a hooker. Always a boss and never a worker. Always a liar, always a thief, and never caught."

I want to believe in prophecies more than policies. I want to listen to poets instead of pollsters. I want prosperity for all rather than profits for some. I want to believe in the people rather than the president.

Viet Thanh Nguyen

A "HOLLA" FROM THE WEST SIDE

Cherríe Moraga

One is responsible to life: It is the small beacon in that terrifying darkness from which we come and to which we shall return. One must negotiate this passage as nobly as possible, for the sake of those who are coming after us.

—James Baldwin, "Down at the Cross"

Dear "Radically Hopeful" Artist:

The closing credits to *Fences*, the film version of August Wilson's play, roll as the mostly black Oakland audience rolls out of the movie house, laughing, talking, and in the good humor of the season. It is a blustery, bright Christmas afternoon. We three remain in our seats—my twenty-three-year-old son to my left and my woman (of twenty years together) to my right. We are what remains of our family for the day, after the grown children and grandchildren have gone on to other family obligations.

I didn't know that Denzel Washington, in the leading

role, had also directed the film. But I hadn't come to the
show for Denzel as much as I had come for Viola Davis, to
hear her say aloud what has always struck me as the most
genuinely feminist line of dialogue in the August Wilson
oeuvre. "From right now . . . this child got a mother. But
you a womanless man."

Still, arriving at that credit line—"Directed by Denzel
Washington"—unexpectedly hits me and hits me hard. I
think, *August finally got what he wanted, and he is too dead
to know of it (consciously at least)*.

I start to say something to that effect to my son and my
woman . . . about August more than ten years dead now . . .
and this play . . . turned movie . . . with these perfect Black
actors . . . and this perfectly irreverent (and utterly rever-
ent) audience, calling out to the dialogue like they were
the words of gospel, spilling from that picture show pulpit.
But I don't get further than a few stuttered words when a
sudden grief rises up in me, like August is my own missing
brother—gone and vindicated all at once because a decade
after his passing his words and work finally return to the
class and color of people who inspired them. Not on Broadway but at the Bayfair Mall theater, on the edge of East
Oakland.

And it is a great llanto I hold inside of me, a cry from the
rafters of the theaters of U.S. America that we—people of
color—hold so, so many stories, just like this, left untold; so,
so many stories that could heal a people if they could reach
a people, make a people feel less crazy to know what they

know and feel what they feel; stories that allow a people to consider upon their lives in a way that might change their lives; stories where the heavens do part on good days to honor our passings.

We will not die uselessly, our art protests.

My woman is a Mexican like me and knows me well enough to leave me alone with the lump of five centuries' silence in my throat. Because I gotta swallow that silence at least long enough to get out of the movie house. But my son is stunned.

"What just happened to you?" he wants to know. His eyes tell me he has witnessed something shift in me, something he cannot place, something he fears for/in me. I cannot speak for a full minute, swallowing, swallowing.

"I just feel sad," I murmur.

"But I can't help you," he implores.

I pause and mean it. "It's okay. You don't have to."

For what I cannot explain is that in that fleeting rush of feeling, I am more alive than I had been in so many months in the slumber of teaching and speeching and schooling and mothering and daughtering and breadwinning and losing in this already Time of Trump. And, you see, there is that two-second moment in the film, which I suddenly remember on the worn heels of my private grief, where Troy, played by Denzel, pulls out his ever-present pint of gin and just before he takes a swig, pauses only long enough to pour a drop of libation into that Pittsburgh steel yard backyard.

And, I can't help but think, *It musta been for August.*

———

In that resides a hope—that you can be a mainstream person of color creating a mainstream film with a mainstream producer and still remember your origins, remember you were a people that preceded and survived slavery and will continue onward. I know this has happened before, but it is also happening again now, and this is what I want for all people of color—the immigrant and refugee, the indigenous and indentured—works that remember and can imagine a livable future where Anglo American "diversity" dies and our cultures thrive.

Mainstream Economics 101: Art Production Under Capitalism:

If there is no "profit" to be made, it will not be made. If there is no "market," there is no means. Chicanos have been writing in English since the southwest became the Southwest, more than a century and a half ago. Still, to this day, what we see of ourselves on TV and in film (with some noble exceptions*) does not reflect a people—a politic perhaps, a joke surely, an introduction to the Mexican American family always—but "us" in all our complexity?—apenas nada, because there simply is not enough opportunity to work at that level. Maybe I also cried seeing *Fences* not because it was perfect but because it had the freedom to be specific. It was August Wilson's point of view in the culturally competent hands of his director and actors. And it had reached la plebe—the people.

---

* Some that come to mind are *Salt of the Earth* (1954), *El Norte* (1983), *La Bamba* (1987), *Quinceañera* (2006), and *A Better Life* (2011).

With the growing visibility of African American work on stage and screen, even utter foolishness, stereotypes, sexist stand-up, and conservative christianities can have their place. Real cultural equity means just that: that our people have the right to be fools, too, just like white folks. Each *individual* work does not have to represent the *whole* race. And in that specificity, real art can happen; in that specificity, an audience member might very well find her own freedom road home.

As a U.S.-born Mexican, educated in English, I have always looked to Black Americans as my trusted artist-ancestors because in most Black artists resides an impassioned resistance to full assimilation (and a daily experience with racism that reminds them not to). Today, as the result of so much laboring in the fields of literature—Morrison, Baldwin, Toni Cade Bambara, Adrienne Kennedy, W. E. B. DuBois, *The Autobiography of Malcolm X, Cane, Meridian, Their Eyes Were Watching God*, Audre Lorde (always Audre)—it appears that, more than ever, a collective consciousness guided by the knowledgeable hand of history is taking hold on the page and stage and screen. I am not a scholar of African American literature or film, but I am their student. And from that perspective, it strikes me that as the Black Lives Matter movement crosses the nation, visionary Black arts—from the streets to the screen—move as its harbinger and in its wake, reaching popular audiences, like the neighborhood folks who showed up at the Bayfair Mall theater on Christmas Day.

There is a renaissance of African-based knowledges (in their myriad multicultural American formations) taking hold of the Black imagination. Indigenous American memory and imaginings are also reconfiguring the text and subtext of Latino and Latina works, from the simplest gesture of spilling the ashes of a mother figure into the waters of her native Puerto Rico in *Water by the Spoonful* to the revolutionary liberation of the Queen Bee in Ricardo Bracho's *Puto* bringing armed struggle and the promise of flowers to a poisoned California Central Valley. The stories are changing, responding to a broader definition of América and of "color." There is the elegant *Moonlight*, directed by Barry Jenkins, where Black drug dealers can be fatherly *and* Cuban at once (yes, Spanish-speaking African Americans *are* part of its diaspora). And where a blue-black boy can return home a queer man behind a golden-grilled smile and allow his head to be held in the open palm of a brother.

All this to say: I am fool enough to believe that storytelling matters; that metaphors make spirits sing; that only art can convince us—in its brutal complexity, in its myriad contradictions, and its nuanced portraiture of love—that we, as human beings, long for meaning in our lives and that this longing ennobles us.

So, at this time with so much burgeoning art—on and off the grid, especially from young folk (YouTube, podcasts, WordPress, and every kind of social media at a pace impossible to keep pace with), we are witnessing a phenomenal "democratization" of access, if you *got* access to the tools. But I am throwback and old enough to recognize the political moment—where broke artists can only imagine getting more broke and with a federal government coming into office bent on our oblivion.

For people of color—from those who dwell in the prison of a powerless poverty to those enraptured by exceptional privilege—our silence serves as the perennial grindstone sharpening the amnesia of white America. As such, our radicalism as artists resides in a shared and vocal awakening and a rigorous literacy campaign regarding the specific historical conditions of one another's colonization and neocolonization and the eruptions of art that resist it. To continue to exclusively understand race in the United States through the black/white lens of the Founding Fathers (i.e., the exploitation, commodification, and enslavement of African Americans alone) is to unwittingly reinforce the genocidal and ethnocidal political structures that have been integral to the very foundation of white supremacy and slavery in this country.

As artists of color, this is the conversation we need to have. To turn to one another in order to locate the connective tissues of silence and wounding in our collective "Body Other"; to become a social and political force of union; to make popular for all our peoples the radical stories of hope needed to be well and right in America. To refuse to position "whiteness" even as an adversary, as the arbiter of our success, our value, our purpose and meaning.

———

Might I speak freely?

These are the things that keep this Chicana up at night.

What does it mean to be a Mexican American and a descendant of Native peoples who were living in the United States before it *was* the United States and still, five hundred years later, be viewed as an immigrant?

How might it feel to be a *Mexican* American and recognize your family's face in virtually every car wash crew, business park custodial team, restaurant cook, dishwasher, and busboy, and in one out of every four stroller-pushing and bucket-bearing domestic workers . . . and then to be told that your own relatives are illegal and a drain on the economy?

Undocumented Mexicans and Central Americans are the twenty-first-century Negro running from Juan Crow. They are children separated from their parents not by the auction block but by the ICE* block. I use this language not to rank oppressions but to make connections; to help you, my reader, to "feel" the weight of it, the wrong of it, the "black" of it.

Okay, then imagine being an eighty-two-year-old Puerto Rican and a feminist and a onetime member of the PSP (the Puerto Rican Socialist Party), and in 2016, you watch your island dropping into a sea of colonial despair and poverty, which is *one* reason why half of the queer folk who died at the club Pulse in Orlando, Florida, were Puerto Rican; but the mainstream and gay media just whitewashed their presence away as LGBTQ. And nobody bothered to ask about their Island.

---

* U.S. Immigration and Customs Enforcement.

And then there are those who remember genocide in their DNA; who witness genocide daily in that raw cut of land called a reservation—where what little *is* left is still *standing as rock* in the winter snow against the frothing open mouths of bulldozers funded by Trump-invested oilers.

So, this is my "holla" from the west side of this continent to say the Wild West still exists, América, with memory banks older than Hollywood, Rushmore, the Alamo, and the California Mission system; memory banks that still contain rivers of knowledge from the Klamath to the Yangtze that, unbeknownst to most, are a critical part of that road map to an American *cultural* revolution.

"The fact of death . . . is the only fact we have," Brother Baldwin reminds us.

August Wilson died, having fulfilled his own mandate to write one play for each decade of the twentieth century. It is a considerable achievement. I did not know August personally, but I did meet him once about twenty years ago. It was just hours after his "The Ground on Which I Stand" keynote at the Theatre Communications Group annual conference at the McCarter Theatre in Princeton. I somewhat timidly approached him, so moved by the eloquence and courage of his words that day. He didn't recognize me as a playwright, a sister "warrior on the cultural battlefield"* of white American theater. I certainly did not expect him

---

* A quotation from his speech.

to. Still, August was half-white like me and perhaps as bitter as me, I imagined, from the impassioned, almost angry insistence in his work. All this mattered (endeared him) to me, his vulnerability, his maybe "weakness" in this way.

And so here I am again, twenty years later, with this small story—now in *your* hands—of one queer Chicana's desire to find a brother from another mother (of color) through the intimate impulses of our shared calling to create.

But it is the fact of death that truly binds, as Baldwin counsels.

To live awake in the face of death: this is the theme that runs beneath and between the lines of this letter and all such letters we hungrily address to one another. We turn to the writings, the images, songs, and tales of others like us (but braver than us) who have walked those trails of tears before us: the enslaved and incarcerated, the displaced and replaced, the boat people and islanders, the refugees and rebels, the dissident and demented, the illuminated. This is the people of color art and art practice we so desperately need, as we so desperately need one another.

Ultimately, what gives me hope (or is it faith?) resides in our shared purpose as artists, especially the elders: that we will be uplifted into a mighty, resonant, and collective "we"—so well versed in the knowledge of death that we, unafraid, will do anything to assure life for generations that follow.

Paz y Pan,
Cherríe Moraga

WHAT I MEAN

Kate Schatz

For these innocent people have no other hope. They are, in effect, still trapped in a history which they do not understand; and until they understand it, they cannot be released from it. They have had to believe for so many years, and for innumerable reasons, that black men are inferior to white men. Many of them, indeed, know better, but, as you will discover, people find it very difficult to act on what they know. To act is to be committed, and to be committed is to be in danger. In this case, the danger, in the minds of most white Americans, is the loss of their identity. Try to imagine how you would feel if you woke up one morning to find the sun shining and all the stars aflame.

—James Baldwin, "My Dungeon Shook—
Letter to My Nephew on the One Hundredth
Anniversary of Emancipation," 1963

Dear White People,

Yes, I'm writing to you. I hope this letter finds you as well as one can be in this world, in this time, this particular speck of millennia.

Did you wake up on the morning of November 9, 2016, and feel, as Baldwin said, as if all the stars were aflame? Like exploding, nuclear hints in the not-too-distant skies? My sun wasn't shining, though—it was as if it had gone out. As if the light were gone. I woke up that morning, and everything felt fucked.

Do you know what I mean?

Many of you feel frightened, horrified, hopeless. You felt you had lost—you were not represented. Your voice was not heard. Your hard work, your vote, your opinions—none of it counted.

If this was a *new* feeling for you, then congratulations: you have lived a very good life.

Congratulations: this is what it is to be white in America.

Do you know what I mean?

In writing to you, white Americans, I am writing to myself as well. When I say *I* and *you* what I really mean is *we*. Because I am one of you. And when I say *white*, I mean—well, let's talk.

I am going to do something in this letter that you might not like. I am going to "make it about race" because, you see, it *is* about race. And we are the ones who made it about race in the first place—our ancestors did this by literally *making race* as a category, as a system to ensure hierarchies of economic, political, and social control. That we benefit from, every day. We made race, and so we need to keep making it about race.

I'm also going to make broad, sweeping statements that generalize our behavior as white people. In many instances, you will think, *Not me!* I ask you to let that go. For example: we just elected Donald Trump. I know *I* didn't vote for him, and I know *you* didn't vote for him, but let's be real here: *we elected him*.

In his letter to his nephew, in *The Fire Next Time*, James Baldwin writes, "You were born where you were born, and faced the future that you faced because you were black and *for no other reason*."

In my letter to you, I offer this: "You were born where you were born, and faced the future that you faced because you were WHITE and *for no other reason*."

Born into the center against which all is measured and defined. Given everything and told very little.

Even the word itself begins like a question—*wh* is the sound we make when we want to know. It is how we begin to learn.

"Wh—who are you?"

"Wh—where am I?"

"Wh—when did it happen?"

"Wh—what does this mean?"

"Wh—why did you do that?"

"Wh—what does it mean to be white?"

No one asks that. We don't know how to answer because, here, in the United States, whiteness is everything. It is air—invisible, constant, what enables us to survive. But it is also artificial: white people, we're born with the oxygen masks strapped to our faces. Breathe in, act normal.

White. It begins like the questions, but there it is, in the middle—the letter *i*. In the center, where whiteness lives. *I*, the rugged (white) individual—the hardy pioneer, the religious freedom seeker, the colonialist, the Manifest Destiny trekker. In other words: my ancestors—our ancestors.

White. The *I* always central, bracketed by beginnings and assumed futures. Then followed by that hard *t*—the tsk of a white woman, the crack of a whip, the sound of the gavel, the handcuffs, the officer's gun.

I, in the center, buffeted and cocooned. Coddled and safe. The norm. The assumptions: that I will live, I will wake up tomorrow, I will not get shot, spit on, pulled over, profiled, pipelined, killed. I didn't do it—*I* wasn't alive then—*I* am not racist.

Dear white Americans, we have nothing and everything in common. Did your family come here from somewhere in Europe? Yes, mine, too. Did they come through Ellis Island, did they raise many children, did they work hard and struggle, did they learn to speak English? Were they seeking a better life? Did they find what they wanted? Yes, mine, too.

Did they fight in wars? Did they own property? Did they own slaves?

Yes.

Mine, too.

Do you know what I mean?

Dear white people, what would it mean to love ourselves so that we may truly love others? What would it mean to fully recognize our whiteness, our privileges, our horrors, and our missteps? To admit and allow that identity-loss danger that Baldwin wrote of, over fifty years ago? To accept and acknowledge—and to vow to resist.

Nothing changes if we just feel shitty about being white. And nothing changes if we refuse to talk about it. The opposite of white pride does not have to be white shame. We can't push it away and pretend it's not us. We are not color blind, we are not post-race, we do not get to reject our whiteness because it makes us feel bad.

We do not swim into the sea, vault off a California cliff, latte in hand, to escape the legacy we are part of. This does not get solved with a Celebration of Diversity Day and a coexist bumper sticker. We can't just Dolezal our way out of it, because to do so would be to employ the very privilege that we want to deny. Do you know what I mean? It is precisely because of our perpetual place in the center that we can even consider a journey to the margins.

In school, we learn white histories, but even those are limited: they are the stories of white power and supremacy, of patriarchal dominance. They do not show us white resistance, white solidarity. I'm not talking about white saviors. I'm not talking about Abraham Lincoln.

Dear white people, we need to know about the Grimké sisters and Lucretia Mott and Julia Ward Howe and Emma Goldman and Jane Addams and Viola Liuzzo and Jessie Daniel Ames and Adrienne Rich and Minnie Bruce Pratt and Polly Spiegel Cowan. It's okay if you don't know these names—they don't teach them. Let's look them up, get to know the names and faces and stories of our ancestors who were not afraid to resist the system designed to benefit them, and who, even as they fought for their rights as women, saw and acknowledged that which their skin afforded them. Good men, too: John Brown and William

Lloyd Garrison and Wendell Phillips and Andrew Good-
man and Michael Henry Schwerner and the Reverend
James Reeb and Richard Loving.

There are heroes in our histories, and they have much
to teach us all.

Dear good white people (you know who you are), I
have a secret to tell you: There is no such thing. There are
only white people who work to do good, just things. You
are an ally because of your actions, not because you say
you are. You're an ally when you call out racist comments,
when you listen and learn, when you work in solidarity with
people of color to dismantle institutional racism, when your
efforts and actions are felt by others. Not just when you
wear a safety pin.

Dear white people, we are going to get it wrong, but we
cannot ever stop trying. This is a challenge because white
people hate being wrong. We're raised to believe that we
know it all, which is especially easy when we're reflected
in every book, every morality tale, every film, every history
lesson.

Those of us who work to do good, just things—we will
try to do right, and we will inevitably disappoint. We will say
it wrong or offend or alienate or misstep or hurt feelings.
We do it all the time. We rarely get told, as the results
are often too much to manage—our defensiveness, our
denial. But when we do get called out? When our gestures/
comments/actions/intentions are met with critique / eye
roll / blank stare / tears / a comment in a Facebook thread?
We cannot run away or shut down or give up or attempt
to neutralize or dismiss someone's lived experience with

a comment (you know the kind—"Ugh why do you have to be so angry all the time?!" "Why do we have to focus on race when we are ALL ONE!"). That is called white fragility, and it is the defensive reaction that occurs at the slightest suggestion of racial stress. White fragility redirects attention onto the emotional state of the white person and shuts down potentially powerful conversations. It is a gut reaction, born of the fear of being wrong, of being racist, of being honest about the fact that, no matter our circumstances, we benefit from white privilege and white supremacy. Every. Single. Day.

So face your shit. Face our shit. Listen. Think. Be open to perspectives that you don't actually agree with. Be open to perspectives on whiteness that come from those who aren't white, because they are the experts. Dear white people, do you have opinions on race in America? Great. Good. Continue to hold and explore these opinions, but make sure they're informed by those who actually live it. People of color experience, daily, what it means to be nonwhite in America, just as women experience, daily, what it is to be not male. They are the ones who can tell you about microaggressions, about the stares and glares and whispers in public, the harassment and the abuse and the ways in which they've been overlooked and passed over and sidelined and silenced. They are the ones to listen to, to learn from. We don't always have to respond or explain or have an answer.

Newsflash, white people: *doing this might make you feel uncomfortable*. Awkward, even. Really shitty. Shame, guilt, helplessness, self-pity—these are all reasonable reactions to truly hearing and seeing the impact of whiteness on people of color. Reasonable, yes—and also 100 percent bullshit if we don't work to move past them, stepping beyond our own guilty sorrows into meaningful action.

So what lies beyond white fragility? White connectedness? White awareness? A white resilience that draws from coalitions, from community beyond itself, from solidarity and a sense of justice and genuine openness to the difficult truths? We have the capacity to grow, to hear, to truly listen to the voices of the world and use our strength for good. Can we do this, white people? Can we brush ourselves off, dry our white tears, and do the work? Spoiler alert: The answer is *yes*. The answer is *we have to*.

White people are a few decades away from being the American minority; here in California, this is already the case. The center cannot hold. Our center, the one that so carefully holds us in great power, measures fellow humans against our skin tone, our physiognomy, our carefully curated histories, our razor-wire borders—that is dissolving as global populations and peoples move around the world (often fleeing war, violence, and environmental devastation).

The American election of 2016 is part of a global fit of white fear, a desperate and deadly shift toward retro nationalism, violent xenophobia, walls, and wars. It was won on the backs of immigrants, of women, of American citizens of color. It was won on fear and desperation, on white anxiety and ignorance—and apathy. White people: we are a problem. Let us please be a solution.

Resistance is urgent; resistance is now. This world, this country, this moment—it requires resilience, steadfastness. It requires hope, love, and a radical commitment to truth and justice. It is a long, hard haul—ask any elder activist, anyone who has spent their life in the Movement, the Struggle—but it is right and necessary work. White people: we who wake up each morning are lucky to be alive. What do we want the world to look like?

Love,
Kate

DEAR MR. ROELL

Boris Fishman

Dear Paul Roell—

I know your name because it appeared in a November 12, 2016, *New York Times* article, shortly after the election, about the loss of 1,400 jobs at the Carrier heating and air-conditioning plant in Indianapolis. (Despite being "plenty profitable," Carrier was moving operations to Mexico because it could get people there to work for a lot less.) That article, written by Nelson D. Schwartz, gave me hope during a period of the greatest despair I've felt about this country since emigrating from the former Soviet Union at the age of nine, in 1988. It was the way so many of the Carrier workers interviewed in the article distinguished their sense of economic disenfranchisement from the racism and bigotry of other Trump supporters:

> Dozens of Burmese immigrants have gone to work at
> the factory in recent years. . . . "It can be hard to com-

municate, but they work very hard," Mr. Maynard [a Carrier team leader who enthusiastically backed Mr. Trump] said. "They don't complain, and I love their work ethic."

And the neighborhoods around Carrier's factory are considerably more diverse than many wealthy New York and San Francisco suburbs, where Democrats dominate. . . . A worker at a plastics factory nearby, Mr. Link noted that a Hispanic family recently moved in next door, and he said he was pleased that blacks and whites now socialize in ways almost unimaginable decades ago. . . .

Mr. Presley, the 59-year-old white Crawfordsville steelworker who voted for Mr. Obama in 2008 and Mr. Trump in 2016, was even more emphatic that racial resentment or ethnic bigotry was not behind his support for Mr. Trump. "I grew up on the West Side of Indianapolis in a racist environment," he said. "But I went to a high school that was 57 percent black, and I played football with a lot of black guys and we became close friends. I learned not to be racist."

But the article also said:

When he drives to work each day before dawn, Mr. Roell passes warehouse after warehouse of giants like Walmart and Kohl's with "Help Wanted" signs outside promising jobs within. The problem is that they typically pay $13 to $15 an hour.

"I guess I could work two full-time shifts a day," he joked.

You may not have been joking, Mr. Roell—that may have been the reporter's inaccurate spin—but seeing that comment took away some of my relief. I'm writing this in an airport where I was brought by a livery driver at 6:30 a.m. I asked him how long he'd been on. Since noon the previous day, he said. In my city, this is true for too many: the Mexican countermen at my local deli, who leave home before dawn and return after dark, and from whom I've never seen anything but a smile in between; the Haitian dishwasher who, also without apparent resentment, washed dishes until midnight and then spent hours cleaning a restaurant where I moonlit as a prep cook last year; my own father, who, at sixty-three, after nearly three decades here, still works double shifts every Monday and many holidays.

Even as their labor and work ethic are sending their children to places like UPenn and Harvard—and representing, to me, the very essence of what it means to be American—and even as I urge you to notice that the "elite" these kids will be forming had its origins in socioeconomic conditions far below yours, I mention this not to browbeat you, Mr. Roell. It did upset me to read another Carrier worker say—in an article in the *Indianapolis Star*, in response to Carrier's offer of multiyear retraining and educational programs, plus financial help—"I've got 13 years in, and I don't really want to start back over." I'm a writer, Mr. Roell— part of that vaunted East Coast urban elite. I have fifteen years "in." Fewer and fewer people touch the kind of literary fiction I write, so that my own layoff from my beloved career—after all these years of working, on average, six and sometimes seven days a week, sometimes for ten hours a day and sometimes for sixteen—is not so hard to imagine. I would feel most fortunate if someone offered to retrain me and pay me something while I did it.

Don't get me wrong—I am not myself if I don't get to write. But bread has to go on the table—my immigrant father, a man who suppressed his artistic talents for a steady paycheck, taught me that. Also, an offer of formal retraining and financial assistance would lend dignity to the new direction—as opposed to blazing my way with little formal support, though with plenty of rejection and doubt, as I had to with writing. That same father of mine has hands of gold: tremendous craft skills that he refused to teach me so I would focus on the kind of studying that would lead to a job "in a suit and tie." It's an old story. But guess what skills I fantasize the most about obtaining? I content myself with volunteer farm labor and handiwork of dubious quality around the apartment, relishing even this small reprieve from the mental exhaustion but physical restlessness of work in a desk chair. But I certainly wouldn't mind knowing how an air conditioner comes together. Uncertainty is also possibility, Mr. Roell—isn't that one of the few American guarantees? Believe me—I know just how uncomfortable the former feels; I've lived without a regular income for twelve years. But if one is willing to weather it and work like hell, one does stand to break through, even in this lopsided America of ours, and as a more resilient, wise, and versatile person for the ordeal. It feels so unfair to have to, doesn't it? And yet, the things I am proudest of within myself came out of adversity, not the opposite.

That said, it is as much a travesty that you must work a double shift to get by as it is that that Haitian dishwasher did. So I mention him to ask why you saw your salvation in Donald Trump instead of in an alliance with people like him. To hang our hopes on the goodwill, threats, and market manipulation of a single man instead of on a political philosophy grounded in common interest and need makes me think of my birthplace, where a sufferer's best hope lies in catching the president's attention during a call-in forum— a system no more evolved than how it was with the czars. This is looking for a handout, not programmatic justice. Aren't handouts why the conservatives vilify liberals?

Please believe that I not only understand but sympathize with part of Donald Trump's appeal. He speaks tough at a time when the world seems full of sharks. As someone who was born in a totalitarian state, sometimes I feel like I understand something many of my fellow liberals don't: there is true evil in the world, and you can't negotiate with it. Sometimes the threat of escalation is worth the projection of force and deterrents. And I don't know whether—despite formative experiences in Indonesia and Kenya, corrupt, repressive, and authoritarian countries—our outgoing president, whose intelligence and spirit I could not admire more, felt the same way. But even this didn't prevent him from eliminating Osama bin Laden, deploying more drone strikes than his predecessor, keeping Guantánamo open, and deporting two million undocumented immigrants. Everything is so frustratingly complex and nuanced, Mr. Roell. Donald Trump tried to hide this during his campaign, but it's one thing to stand up to evil and another to demonize and scapegoat so we don't have to feel responsible or so the real villains remain in the shadows. What kind of nationalist strongman is ready to brush off the interference of a foreign power in our internal politics? This isn't nationalism or strength; it's such hatred of domestic rivals that Donald Trump prefers to find common cause with foreign forces.

Because I know some of my fellow liberals address people like you with deferential-sounding exhortation (with you, too, they try to be politically correct) that sometimes poorly masks their condescension, exasperation, and, ultimately, incomprehension, I would like to do neither, but rather speak directly, as I believe adults must, as I believe is far more respectful: Beware a sense of entitlement, Mr. Roell. Beware victimhood. And beware finger-pointing, lest the finger point back at you—for a long time, conservatives have been saying that entitlement and victimhood are the specialty of the left. This is how Middle Eastern dictators justify their corruption and the impoverishment of their people—the Israelis are to blame for it. This is how Robert Mugabe keeps Zimbabwe on its knees—the West is responsible. For the Russians, who want only peace and love, the Americans are to blame. If you believe in American exceptionalism, Mr. Roell, you can see: we're not so exceptional, after all.

Beware easy answers, Mr. Roell. Anyone can pander to sentiment to cloak the painful facts: in our case, that technology and automation are responsible for far more job loss than globalization. (Perhaps we should deport Silicon Valley.) And the nuanced facts: even when globalization is to blame, to undo it means not only bringing Carrier jobs back; it means twenty-five-dollar T-shirts at the clothing store. You can't have one without the other, as you can't have healthy food without a high price tag. But nuance is unwelcome in our political discourse. A consideration of the whole picture—unwelcome. Unfortunately, all that's left then are lies.

My favorite thing about the Carrier article was its lead photo: a black woman and a white woman, both Carrier employees, both under the same ax. The Republican Party has cleaved the white working class from working-class people of color by exploiting a weakness to which co-sufferers are especially prone. I see it among my people—ex-Soviet immigrants—so many of whom refuse to see their past selves in present-day refugees precisely because *they* were refugees once.

Beware being used, Mr. Roell. You have been told: *You are not like them.* But you are, Mr. Roell—what proves it more than the double shift you must contemplate? As I am like you—for the same reason. Please know I see our salvation in the Democratic Party, in centrist liberalism, hardly more than in the Republican. Our salvation lies in our grasping the connection between us and the power it confers, and in understanding the self-deceit involved in handing it over to a man like Donald Trump (even as, I agree, Hillary Clinton would not have shifted the bedrock of what ails us). Who, then; and how; and in what free time? I don't know, Mr. Roell. But I would like to meet you and figure it out together.

With respect, frustration, curiosity, anger,
empathy, and goodwill,
Boris Fishman

AN ADDENDUM TO MY FELLOW LIBERALS:

In the months before the election, I started thinking of writing an opinion piece called "Want to Beat Trump? Try to Understand the People Who Support Him. Hell, *I* Support Some of Him. Why?" This perspective didn't find much resonance in the liberal circles of Manhattan and Brooklyn—journalists, writers, and the like—that I frequent. Despite months of looking, I never managed to meet a liberal New Yorker who thought of Trump supporters as anything other than an undifferentiated bloc of subhuman troglodytes. It made me question our liberalism, a liberalism that came to feel like it believes in the right things only as long as they have to do with the right people. (Sound familiar?) Can liberalism remain incurious and nose-holding and remain liberalism? In recent years, liberal tactics sometimes have seemed to share more with Donald Trump than Nelson Mandela. Maybe the exit polls failed because Trump supporters were embarrassed to admit they were voting for him—because that might mean they would get strung up on some correctly liberal blog as hick racists.

Whether for reasons of temperament or political miscalculation, we were led by someone who didn't address the complaints of people like Paul Roell with something more detailed, dogged, and heartfelt than bromides. ("I want to be *everyone's* president.") Our candidate did not dignify their grievances; did not push into their midst; did not try to cleave the Roells, Links, Maynards, and Presleys from the misogynists, supremacists, bigots, and racists. Never got angry, never forcefully but uncondescendingly called out—as anti-American, as morally evil, as lies and here's why—and scrupulously dismantled the manipulations and falsehoods of the other side. And when the one Clinton firebrand—Bill—finally spoke some truth, about Obama-care (a disaster for this self-employed person), he got eviscerated by our side.

If this election can inspire us to anything, liberal friends, let's not only redouble our efforts to advocate for the forgotten, the unprotected, and the newly threatened. Let's also do the last thing I know so many of us are planning to do. Let's get out of our comfort zones. Let's leave New York and its groupthink. Let's lose our certainty—perhaps our arrogance. Let's get off social media and its sanction of the kind of condescension and scorn we would never permit ourselves face-to-face. Let's be the person who disagrees at the dinner party. Let's get into the country. Let's talk to people who are nothing like us—politically. (I mean, of course, the Paul Roells, not the bigots.) Let's try to understand them on their terms. We are listening to them as little as they are listening to us. And I'm not sure who stopped listening first.

WHILE YOU ARE STANDING

Karen Joy Fowler

To the protectors at Standing Rock—

Something inside me died on Election Night, and that something was my faith. For more than sixty years, deep in my heart, I did believe that we would overcome someday. And then, in a matter of hours, on the evening of November 8, 2016, I stopped believing.

When the results posted, my president told me that I could still have faith in our institutions, which had lasted in fair weather and foul for two hundred years. But let's do a quick inventory.

1) Obviously, he can't have meant the presidency itself, which in my lifetime has been held too often by crooks and criminals. Sometimes the office may elevate the man; more often, the man degrades the office. We are about to be governed by an unstable, unintelligent and unaccomplished, avaricious and vicious, clownish, lying, cheating, self-obsessed sexual predator. This is a shame from which the office and the nation will never recover.

2) But perhaps he meant our legal system. We are, after all, often told that we are a nation of laws.

Except that we are not. Apparently, our legal structures are quite fragile, since prosecuting the rich and powerful is always deemed too destabilizing to be attempted. Better just to admonish them and let them go. Though even an admonishment may be too much; better not to even mention it. Congress is currently debating just how many laws the president should be asked to follow if he's not so inclined. The rich and powerful will never face the same legal sanctions as the poor and unconnected. The law is for chumps.

While the Supreme Court is for the sort of people known as corporations. I believed in the Supreme Court for a long time, starting with the unanimous decision in *Brown v. Board of Education*, so giving that up hurt me a lot. But with the judicial coup of 2000, the Supremes proved themselves just as motivated by partisan politics as Congress is. Congress recently acknowledged this by blatantly cheating President Obama out of his final court pick.

3) Congress is a cruel joke. I don't think anyone disagrees.

4) Four is for the Fourth Estate. During my lifetime, they've had some fine moments. We learn about these when we study history, because history is where they are. For several years now, the chase for ratings, the inability to call a lie a lie for fear of appearing partisan, the focus on the campaign rather than the issues, the complete abrogation of any responsibility to inform ordinary people of how particular policies may impact their lives and the unwillingness and lack of resources necessary to do the long, hard work of discovering the truth have rendered the media malig-

nant. Fox will always be Fox, but CNN's hiring of Corey Lewandowski, who worked for the Trump campaign before, during, and after his tenure, and MSNBC's chummy phone calls between Trump and *Morning Joe* represent memorable lows. What's best for television news is what's bad for the country. You heard that straight from the mouth of CBS CEO Les Moonves.

Print media are only intermittently better, and the Internet is awash in fake news. There remain a few reporters you can trust, and thank god for them. But no one on either side of the aisle thinks that the media will do the job a democracy requires them to do.

5) The two-party system? Only works if both parties believe in democracy. When one party applies itself vigorously to lying to the electorate, suppressing the vote, and gerrymandering the districts, there is no democracy. Elections may still be held, but there is no democracy. Just look at the mad, sad state of North Carolina.

(And this is a small point by comparison, but why do Republicans persist in substituting *Democrat*, with its *rat* ending, when *Democratic* would be correct? Because they want us to know, in every word they speak, how much they hold us in contempt. In my lifetime, the Republicans have never accepted a Democratic president as legitimate, no matter how many people vote for him [or her.])

Meanwhile, the only thing the Democratic Party seems capable of is a graceful loss. This quick impulse to concede is a mighty betrayal of the people who depend on them. The Democrats will take my money and ask for more—I get multiple requests every single day—but they will not fight for me.

6) Money brings us directly to elections.

Thanks to the Supreme Court, which has decided that the Constitution gives more voice to rich people than poor, elections are now flooded with secret monies and the inevitable corruption that follows. Bribery has been legalized.

Thanks to the Supreme Court, the Republican Party is now free to reprise Jim Crow in a dozen creative ways in order to prevent undesirables from voting. Republicans can bleat all they like about voter fraud (actively encouraging a lack of faith in the electoral results while they do so), but their actual motives are transparent. Sometimes they forget to use their inside voices and admit to it.

Besides, much as we dislike asking them, there are genuine questions about the integrity of the ballot count and the security of our voting machines.

7) Back when I was taking high school civics, much was made of how cleverly the Founding Fathers had calibrated a balance of powers. But the electoral process is so degraded that the minority party has managed to exploit its way into holding all branches. Although many more people voted against Trump than for him, we find ourselves now under an administration without balance and without check.

8) The CIA has always been a lawless gang of thugs. Have gun, will travel. Endanger American profits? Will kill.

9) The FBI serves the FBI and interferes in our elections as openly as Russia does.

10) Our local police forces have been militarized and too often terrorize and murder the citizens they are supposed to protect.

11) The public schools are being deliberately destroyed under the guise of privatization.

12) The libraries are holding on by their fingernails. (Though I do still love the libraries.)

So, it has been many years since I had any faith in our institutions. That eagle has flown. Instead, my faith was in the general decency and generosity of the majority of Americans. (Other people in other nations, too.) I believed that most people were basically good.

And because of this, I had faith in activism. I believed in people working together to make the world more equitable. I believed in witness, in persistence, in resistance. I believed in the long moral arc of the universe bending toward justice.

It was easy initially to believe this, because I came of political age during the civil rights movement. I kept that belief throughout the antiwar movement, the women's movement, gay rights, animal rights, Occupy, and Black Lives Matter.

I also saw that actions could have unintended consequences. Our defeat in Vietnam led to every American war that followed. The women's movement strengthened and armed the antiabortionists. Ronald Reagan deliberately chose the student activists as the antagonists who, properly caricatured and vilified, would take him all the way to the presidency. (There can be considerable disagreement as to the day the world began to end. But those of us of a certain age remember how quickly and triumphantly Reagan removed the solar panels from the Carter White House.) And still I believed we were moving, in fits and starts, toward justice.

That belief is one of the many things I lost on November 8. I woke on the ninth to the realization of how quickly the work of my lifetime could be wiped away. Four years should be enough to undo it entirely.

I saw that I had overestimated the goodness of ordinary people.

I saw that men who care about nothing but money will always rule the world. We protestors have been opposing the likes of Dick Cheney, Donald Rumsfeld, and Henry Kissinger my whole life. Not just the likes of them, either, but the actual *them* of them. They will never go away, and they will always have much more power than you and I.

When I read about you gathering at Standing Rock to halt the construction of the Dakota Access Pipeline, when I read how you were met with mace and dogs, tear gas and water cannons, when journalists were among those arrested and injuries were blamed on the activists who'd suffered them, I thought, yes, I've seen this show before.

I will see it again. I know how it ends. The Bundys of the world will be found innocent. The Snowdens will not. Our public lands will be sold and plundered along with our public schools. We will lose the inestimable treasure of rhinos and whales, frogs and bees. We will never have a victory that can be made to last, but when the cheetahs are gone, they are gone forever. And I saw that I was tired.

But you were not.

I read a postelection blog post by the great Ursula K. Le Guin that said that we should stop using the metaphors of war. We should not think in terms of enemies and battles, because such thoughts, in themselves, change who we are.

We need to be like water, she wrote. Water can be "divided and defiled, yet continues to be itself and to always go in the direction it must go."

The water metaphor takes me many places. It takes me to the melting Arctic ice and the rising sea levels. It takes me to the Gulf of Mexico and *Deepwater Horizon*. It takes me to the toxic tap water of Flint, Michigan, and Corpus Christi, Texas, and Hoosick Falls, New York. It takes me to the water cannons used against you. But it also takes me to you, oh water protectors!

All we have are our words and our bodies. We used our words in the last election. We were as eloquent and persuasive as we could be and still it ended with this cartoon villain as president.

The water metaphor is an embodied one. It says that we must get off the Internet and put our bodies into the world again. We must talk others in our communities into doing the same. When our national government and our department of justice are hostile to us, when our actual physical presence is required, our focus necessarily becomes local.

Once more, and then again, and then again, we must, as Mario Savio told us back in 1964, put our "bodies upon the gears and upon the wheels, upon the levers" of the machine. We must learn or relearn the practice of nonviolence, which has never been a yielding, passive policy, but requires enormous courage and the likelihood of much sacrifice. We will need to do all the things you've been doing for many months now. Maybe we will need to be like water. Certainly, we will need to be like you.

I was recently at an event with Grace Dillon, a professor in the Indigenous Nations Studies program at Portland State and a woman of the Anishinaabe people. "Five hundred years of struggle," she told me when we said good-bye, and then she hugged me and laughed, because laughing is what Grace Dillon does; it's her superpower.

Five hundred years.

In which the men with money have always had more voice and the men who only value money will persist in that until finally they take the whole planet down with them.

But I have decided to persist as well. I look to you, the water protectors at Standing Rock. How good to me, how necessary, you have been. In you, I have found some measure of that lost faith again. You need allies. I will not sit down while you are standing.

I understand that you have won no victories that cannot be taken back. A century will not heal the natural world from the damage that can be done in a day. The odds and the calendar are against us. But I am not as tired as I thought.

And for that and so much else, I thank you.
From deep in my heart,
Karen

TO THE WOMAN STANDING IN LINE AT THE STORE,

Elmaz Abinader

You are ahead of me, without a grocery basket, hugging two acorn squash, four ears of corn, and a can of oatmeal. You're wearing jeans and an open maroon sweater, hitched up on the side where your purse is dangling. Your friend is leaning on the red shopping cart, her face close to a bouquet—some of the flowers are unnaturally colored—a sea-turquoise blue daisy, and a mango-orange carnation, similar to the color of her hair.

You are conversing in Spanish, slowly and measured, as if you know I am eavesdropping and need time to adjust to your accent, re-key my ears. My basket holds choices for my upcoming dinner party: large filleted salmon, crisp organic asparagus, Belgian endive that will be layered with goat cheese and sun-dried tomatoes. My list has been completed, my plans are arranged; my party will unfold as precisely as I have strategized it, I think.

I am not trying to listen to you, but your whisper, while urgent and private, is within my earshot, and the words tortura and cárcel command my attention. I want to know if you are telling a story about yourself or someone else. Where was this jail? What kind of torture? You are steady in your telling, sparing the graphic details. As you speak, you don't change expression. "Pasé diez años allí, y luego me soltaron. Mi madre tenía a mis hijos en Buenos Aires; ya no me conocían. Entonces me fui, y vine acá." Your body stays still as you describe your trip from your country to Oakland, after a decade in prison, after giving up your children.

Had I been farther back in the line or somewhere across the store, you would have been another fortysomething woman, just off work at Kaiser or my credit union, picking up something for dinner. And if I'd imagined your conversation from far off, it might have been about your plumbing issues or a hair appointment on Saturday. But I was near, a witness to the story of your time in prison, when you were tortured, leaving your shoulder frozen in one position.

You are the woman standing in line at the grocery store, but you are also walking your kid to the school near my house; you might be cleaning the neighbor's bathroom, or teaching a singing class, translating court documents, or counseling community college students. Not all of you are former prisoners—some of you are refugees from countries that have collapsed or became dangerous to live in. Many of you are dreamers, hoping to have more than nothing, and something to send back. You have walked across borders, fled a civil war; escaped the ruling political party or the fanatic religious movement. Some of you came for an education and never went back.

You are, for me, my sittu, who, during the fading Ottoman Empire in Lebanon in 1916, tucked the last of your jewelry into your waistband, crawled through shrubbery, below sight line, up and down mountainsides, to trade everything you had for rice, flour, and beans. You fed my mother and her sister at any cost. You traveled with them barefoot, along the stony paths from the mountains to the city, your belongings in a bundle on your head, to make that two-year journey that ended in Pennsylvania.

And a half century later, your granddaughter, my cousin, sat in the dark in a fallout shelter while the city burned above her head. Her eyes cat-widened, and her hearing dulled to the sounds of street blasts and missile cries. She is a mother in New Jersey now, conducting training for a software company. She is also a woman standing in line.

The graduate student in my writing class who had to endure checkpoints and searches every day she moved through her town, the woman in my writing group who has lived under two dictatorships, the mother of my student who escaped Pol Pot, make coffee and peel oranges, fold laundry and watch TV. The Filipina Lola, once a comfort woman for the Japanese soldiers, cradles her granddaughter in a stuffed chair in Daly City. My friend's sister with more than fifty pieces of shrapnel in her body is now a master chef and magazine editor.

———

You, women in line at the store, arrive every day—apprehensively or confidently. Refugees from that world you knew, no matter how painful. Most of you hold your stories inside, while you transform outside to a new person, taking cues from television, and you find other women like you fumbling with a new society. You stuff down the pain of buried children, your destroyed home, and lost language while you fill out forms and registration cards, sign leases, and take a driving test.

Dear Woman Standing in Line at the Store,

I want to be attentive to you. Listen well to your whispers, find clues in the way you raise your hand while you talk, or tuck your blouse into your waistband and lower your head. Hear the endearments you kneel to pour in the ears of your children, along with the instructions and the messages. I don't want to unearth your journey out of greed or curiosity; but as a way to know you and let your story tell me who I might be.

I am not courageous enough to put my back to my life, to whom I know, what I do, and how I live. I cannot imagine less in my life or separate from whom I love. I cannot fathom riding the boats that carried you, waving good-bye to my grandmother, paying the man who forged the papers, begging the minister to sign for the visa, sneaking onto the train holding my child, eating food from other people's hands; whispering endless prayers that echoed the number of footprints.

As you walk the same city I do—the path around the lake, the redwood trails, the crisscross of parking lots and neighborhoods—I try to recognize you. Sometimes I do, from your accent, or your hijab, your sari, your habit of walking exactly twenty times around the block wearing a wide-brimmed hat, the spices you smell with disappointment and the loads you pull behind you.

Many of us have not learned how to lose something. But you know, woman standing in line, that the acorn squash you hold measures heartbeats as you move from one world to the next, never betraying the spot where your life tore in two. I can see there is a story under your skin, and I take courage from the steadiness of your breathing. Pray that the particles of hopefulness that brought you here will lift into the air and we can inhale them into our systems and they ease our journeys and yours, too.

DEAR MILLENNIALS

Aya de León

Dear Millennials,

We weren't really lying, because we believed it at the time. We told you to work hard in school as young people. We buried you in homework. When you wanted to spend time with your friends, we acted like you were throwing away your future. All with the promise that if you graduated from a good college, you'd be set for life.

We told many of you that you weren't college material. We watched others of you try to go to college, and it didn't work out. We sighed. No good life for you. Because college was the gateway to all nice things. *Focus on your studies, and don't rack up credit card debt. Student loans? That's different. Educational debt pays for itself.* We weren't really lying, because we believed it at the time.

College used to be something only owning-class white men could afford. So if others managed to get those degrees, it put them on an elite track. But as increasing numbers of the masses gain access to higher education, there's no simultaneous increase in the number of professional, living-wage jobs for them after they graduate. The system originally designed to benefit the minds and futures of wealthy young white men can't be effortlessly shifted to work for women, people of color, and poor / working-class folks. People of color go to college and feel daily the slice of microaggressions. Poor and working-class kids go to college and get the message that they are intellectually inferior. Young women go to college and get sexually harassed and assaulted. The traumas of these communities in higher education betray the roots of the institution and those for whom it was originally designed to work.

We older folks don't know how to divest from the myth, so we grin and say, *Just keep at it!* during your despair-filled job searches with your bachelor's/master's/PhDs. We even have the nerve to blame those of you who didn't go to college, when you face an even bleaker employment picture. *See? If only you'd gone to college, you could compete with a hundred other qualified applicants for that one interesting, living-wage job.* We promised that your hard work would pay off. We thought we were telling the truth.

Another big lie is that we know. We know what's best for you. We know what you should do with your lives. With your money. We definitely know that you should slow it down in your sex lives.

The truth is not that we know. The truth is that we worry. We worry about your choices, because we're anxious about our own choices. Our own finances. Our own debt. Our own frustrated career aspirations. Our own love and sex lives.

And then there was voting. We thought we could bully you into our voting patterns. We dismissed your commitment to a higher standard of social justice as naïve and unrealistic. And, if you were female, we feminist-shamed you for disloyalty to the female candidate. On behalf of all older adults, I want to say you didn't deserve any of this. Whether or not we agree with you, we need to respect you and, above all, not just come to you to talk when we want something (like your vote). We need to listen more to the stories of your lives and your ideas on how to change things. We need to be more honest and not just share our success stories, but also our fuckups and current struggles.

Here's some honesty. Do you have any idea how much you scare us? Your candor in relationships freaks us out. *Polyamory? Good lord, can't you just lie, sneak, and cheat like normal people?* Your trigger warnings trigger us. *Disclosing your trauma publicly? Yikes! Keep a lid on that. Pretend everything's okay and go cry by yourself in the bathroom like we do.*

So here's the truth. We—as older generations—are anxious and depressed as hell. We're numb, isolated. We've gotten used to the lives we settled for. Even though our choices aren't even available to your generation, still we push these myths as your only options. Your high aspirations scare us and remind us of all the places where we gave up.

But here's what I do know: you're not the future, you're the present. You're the key that allows progressive whites and people of color to constitute a New American Majority[1] that can win any national election, as long as you vote.

Two days after the election, I walked into my college classroom. We were all incredibly upset. We just talked. I tried to be a voice of hope. Our peoples have lived through brutal times before. As someone who lived through the Reagan and the Bush (both father and son) years, I can testify to the fact that we have survived presidential incompetence and mean-spiritedness and corruption. And when I look to my ancestors, I know we have survived active Indigenous genocide and eras in which black lives weren't even classified as fully human under the law. And yet people of conscience fought to change that, and we continue to fight to erase all the cultural vestiges of those legacies, from Standing Rock to the Movement for Black Lives—we had our work cut out for us, even before Trump.

The one gift of his presidency is clarity. Racism, misogyny, and xenophobia are alive and dangerous. And we have a lesson to learn from Trump. He didn't win with the usual Republican strategy of euphemism. He won with crass boldness. Let us learn to be even bolder in our resistance to Trump's racism, sexism, classism, homophobia, transphobia, ableism, and xenophobia. Our boldest move is to build a lasting coalition movement of all these targeted communities that can organize the dissent in this country into a force for deep and permanent change. A progressive coalition that is led by working-class folks who are *both* white and people of color.

We have a chance to do this in 2018 and 2020, but really, we have a chance to do this every day. One of the biggest surprises of the Trump campaign was how it defied all the rules and expectations. So we need to live lives that defy all the rules. We may look back and see Trump as the alarm clock that woke up our nation to the threat, and we rallied to defeat not only him but also everything he stands for. We may look back and see the Trump era as a brutal time that caused great damage and took many lives, worldwide. But I believe—I must have faith—that we, as a nation, will survive and be able to look back.

There is a great deal of despair right now among us progressives. And while there truly are present-time dangers, each one of us is likely triggered about painful issues from our early lives. When have we felt the most helpless? Overwhelmed? Bereft?

When I was born, my young parents were unprepared in many ways. As a small child, I recall my father raising his voice at my mother. Not an earth-shattering yell by adult standards, but to the very young, a voice raised at all in anger is terrifying. Since the election, I have experienced the terror of that little version of myself. The world seemed like such a scary place if this angry guy had so much power. No wonder Trump pushes my buttons. This nation's president symbolizes the archetype of the dream father / nightmare father with the power to affect our lives for better or worse. But I am no longer a small child, and I know now what that very young version of myself didn't know: this man's reign will end. In the point of view of the child, the reach of the yelling man seems endless. We need to take this opportunity to heal those childhood places and draw ourselves up into the fullness of our power.

In my classroom, two days after the election, I drew great strength from something one of my students said. She identifies as a blXicana womxn, and is a survivor of profound childhood sexual trauma. She had written about these experiences throughout the semester, with a boldness and clarity that reflected years of healing work. So when she spoke about Trump, she also testified to her resilience. She had come up against violence that was designed to kill her, to crush her spirit. She had not only survived but had committed herself to continue fighting for her life. She carried a deep belief in herself. While she was enraged and concerned about Trump's election, she was committed to fight for her people, because she had already survived that which was unbearable.

In these coming years, we need to be just that clear about what buttons get pushed for us. We need to fight and scream and cry our way out of those early traumas and release those recordings of helplessness and despair. Even in the midst of a Trump administration, we need to take inspiration from survivors to take back our lives and take charge of our country.

With every devastating executive order and every dangerous piece of legislation that may happen in this era, we need to dig for that core of resilience. We are part of a movement that is building power, not isolated individuals getting crushed by something bigger than we are.

Our isolation is dangerous. We cannot stand up to this president alone. We need each other, and we need to learn to have strong networks of relationships, not just with lovers and romantic partners but with friends, family, and communities. We need to learn how to connect authentically, stay connected, and develop the relationship skills to maintain those connections under pressure. In the coming years, some of us may lose our jobs, our housing, our healthcare, our green cards, our places in schools. Our survival depends upon our ability to build interdependent communities that share resources and care for each other.

So many of the rules of our economy and society have been suspended. There is no safe, reliable career path anymore. So if you have a passion for something, pursue it—even if the path to a *real job* is unclear. Art, writing, music, theater, teaching, youth work, activism, community organizing. But if you don't have a clear passion or path, don't just do what's expected. I regularly discourage my students from applying to med school and law school unless they're excited about being doctors and lawyers. Now is not the time to fake it. If you don't know, spend some time getting to know yourself and what you like to do. And whatever your career path, one of the best things you can do to ensure your future is to be a politically engaged citizen at every level: electoral politics, community activism, and direct action. I challenge my students to stop focusing on finding the *right* thing to do with your life—school, career, marriage—and instead focus on the *next* thing you want to do, as well as building the community of *people* you want to have in your life. Many older adults accomplished our life goals by embracing individualism and neglecting relationships. Let us be a cautionary tale.

Part of our learning here is about how strategies that worked for our generation don't work for you or work differently. We pushed you toward college, because that worked for us. And college had a shadow we hadn't predicted. Women and people of color stormed the barricades of academia in the late '60s and '70s. We criticized the canon, and we deconstructed higher education's Eurocentrism, male domination, Christian hegemony, and the preoccupation with the wealthy. We sharpened our tools of critique on institutions of power and then fought for them to be institutionalized in the curriculum. From the '70s to the '90s, these were tools of radicalism, and these tools are still needed to critique entrenched privileges in institutions of power. And in your excellence, your generation also learned to use these tools of critique on each other. Radical spaces in colleges taught deconstruction without teaching how to build and create and generate. You spoke hard truths to power, but you also spoke hard truths to peers. And these tools created a culture where young people of conscience are often afraid to act and afraid to generate. Afraid their unacknowledged privilege will show. Afraid to offend.

In progressive communities, taking action or leadership or generating new ideas happens under threat of harsh reads, under fears of humiliation or excommunication. We unwittingly gave you the means to create a culture where everyone waits on the sidelines for someone else to say or do something. Everyone is a critic, and it's unsafe to step up with our imperfections. So instead of a culture of shared vulnerability in building new possibilities, instead of a culture where people try and fail and celebrate the attempt, we have unwittingly created a culture where many feel inhibited by fear and inaction until and unless they are perfect.

So your critiques of Hillary were principled and on point, but we weren't able to contextualize these imperfections.

Bernie promised a revolution that hadn't been built yet. We needed to promise to build it together. Hillary didn't require a revolution, because her vision wasn't revolutionary. But it was *possible*. Yet we progressives had handed you the very tools with which you would critique what was possible in favor of what was perfect. You couldn't see Hillary as creating the preferable but imperfect conditions in which *you* would act. Because you were taught to wait on the sidelines for someone beyond criticism.

We needed to have a conversation about incremental change. We needed to sell a Hillary presidency—not as a historic end in itself, but rather as creating a set of conditions in which we would fight for everything else we wanted. And we needed to pledge ourselves to keep fighting. We needed to promise that we wouldn't abandon you in your serious struggles and go back to our settled lives under a business-as-usual Democratic president.

And, of course, your standards were high. Many of you came of age under our first black president. Obama was a miracle. A fluke. We couldn't replicate him. We tried to say that Hillary becoming the first woman president would be like Obama becoming the first African American president. But it wasn't the same. Obama was a new senator. He hadn't had to compromise in the same ways Hillary had. Whether we blame her compromises on sexism or her personal failings, we never told the whole truth. We couldn't replicate Obama because the system isn't set up to produce Obamas. He was an outlier. The system could barely even produce a Hillary. We wanted a woman president following a black president. We wanted to ride a wave of change, when in fact, we were getting pulled by an undertow of backlash. Perhaps in hindsight, the possibility of deeply flawed Hillary looks so much more appealing than she did on November 7.

I am not suggesting that we shouldn't use critical-thinking tools. Rather, I am suggesting that we learn to generate and critique in equal measure. Further, I'm suggesting that we don't critique our allies with the same sharp objects with which we critique our enemies. And I am also suggesting that we become much more selective about whom we label an enemy, and much less selective about who we think has the potential to be in coalition with us. Our critique of those in coalition needs to leave room to move forward together, as opposed to leaving only scorched earth. My generation of progressives embraced the words of Audre Lorde: "The master's tools will never dismantle the master's house."[2] My caution for this generation is as follows: *in the midst of dismantling the master's house, we must be careful not to bring those sharp tools into our own house.*

I am the mother of a child in elementary school. The most fertile spaces for her learning are those that leave room to make mistakes and try again without shame or punishment. As progressives, we need to shape-shift from sideline critics who react to the mainstream into a force that is prepared to take power and govern. I, for one, am joining the push to make the Democrats a bolder party for social justice and the working class. But there are many good strategies that can work together and succeed. In order to win, we need to be willing to risk, envision, and create, try, fail, and try again. We need to develop a space for leadership development that balances forgiveness with accountability. Only then can we move from being people who criticize power to those who are prepared to wield it to create the just and caring world we envision.

We older generations haven't built the world you deserve. We wish we had, but we haven't. We often fall back on criticizing you when you make different choices about how to navigate the world's imperfections. So on behalf of older adults who have lectured when we should have listened, and dictated when we should have disclosed, I want to offer an apology. We did our best, but you deserve better. Can you forgive us? I know we've broken our promises. We didn't mean to hurt you. We weren't really lying because, crazy as it sounds now, we believed it at the time.

I hope that this devastating loss at the national level has shaken us all out of denial and shown us what really matters. You millennials are an incredibly important generation. Your fierceness, your voices, your willfulness, your high expectations. We need you. We love you. We need each other.

In power and love,
Aya

Thanks to all the millennials who contributed their brilliance directly and indirectly to this article: Thea Matthews, Nina Goldman, Sasha Gayle-Schneider, Coco Peila, Alicia Raquel, and Jessica Byrd.

Notes

1. Steve Phillips, *Brown Is the New White: How the Demographic Revolution Has Created a New American Majority* (New York: New Press, 2016).

2. Audre Lorde, "The Master's Tools Will Never Dismantle the Master's House," in *This Bridge Called My Back: Writings By Radical Women of Color*, eds. Cherríe Moraga and Gloria Anzaldúa (New York: Kitchen Table Press, 1981).

IS THERE NO HOPE?

Jane Smiley

Dear Fellow Baby Boomers,

Back in the late '60s, I knew a lot of Marxists. For the most part, they were young, good looking, and smarter than their fellow students (many of whom were legacy admits). When they got to the Ivy League from their middle- and working-class (I had never heard that phrase before then) backgrounds, they were shocked to discover the wealth and the luxury behind the gates. Here they had thought this was a country based on freedom and equality! The conversations that struck me then, and that I remember now, were about "effecting change." As a natural liberal, avid novel reader, and survivor of the Cold War, I argued for incremental improvement based on shared humanity and goodwill. I didn't actually believe that "the ruling class" was evil, only ignorant. If they were to meet the people who were suffering, they would . . .

Raise the minimum wage? I had a minimum-wage job at

the time. I was making $1.75 an hour. Today, that would be two dollars more than the current minimum wage in that state.

Make sure everyone could vote? Why wouldn't they? Didn't they believe in constitutional rights?

Improve public education? Well, maybe that didn't need improvement, since my smart friends were publicly educated, and if you didn't get a scholarship to a fancy school, you could attend an innovative land-grant university like Iowa State or parts of Cornell for next to nothing.

Improve race relations? Weren't we well on the way, thanks to Martin Luther King and Rosa Parks?

I knew someone in "the ruling class": my stepfather. He was a saint.

My friends were not quite ready to wreck the system, nor were they armed, but they argued for doing it. The case they made was that incremental change didn't fix the power structure, that doing what I wanted to do was essentially a form of bribery that would put off the inevitable revolution. When I pointed out that two revolutions we knew about at the time, the Russian and the Chinese ones, hadn't worked out very well, they would say, "Mistakes were made." They didn't say how they would avoid those mistakes. They were twenty years old. They had no idea. And neither did I.

Nor did I know that Marx himself was on my side—he once said that the United States might be won over to Marxism through elections.

Nor did I know what I later learned in one of my favorite

books, *The Great Wave* by David Hackett Fischer—that the peasantry, or the working class, or the mob, or the plebs, or the huddled masses do have brief periods of power and prosperity, but only after plagues, famines, and wars, when they become more scarce and therefore more valuable.

It seemed to me at the time that we should make use of our educations to follow our passions. Mine was literature. I followed it, both on foot and in books. I might say that I was right to do so, but at the same time, I have watched the ideals that took me out of the Midwest to that treasure house of books and professors and friends crumble one at a time. I am a little like an earthquake survivor who happens to avoid the falling walls and opening rifts.

There are plenty of people who did not survive, or only barely survived, the economic and political earthquakes of the last forty-five years, and by electing Donald Trump, with the help of former KGB officer Vladimir Putin, they have chosen the option my Marxist comrades argued for in the summer of 1969—wreck the system, assume something better will emerge, because what could go wrong, after all? We have our feelings to back us up.

Donald Trump knows where *his* sympathies lie, and that is with his own businesses and his own wealth. He is not a leader and not a patriot and not a bureaucrat. He is a self-centered fool who is being manipulated by the people he knows into forming exactly the ruthless, Ayn Randian sort of megacapitalist government that the corporatocracy has been slavering for since 1980. All of those things that I thought the ruling class (and that is what they are, now) would do just out of normal human decency and connection, they have chosen not to do—they have not raised the minimum wage in line with inflation, they have not guaranteed the right to vote, they have not improved race relations, nor have they funded public education, repaired the infrastructure, reached across the aisle. And, worst of all, they have denied the science of climate change in the face of daily, monthly, and seasonal environmental alerts. They have sat idly by as the natural world fades away, as animals are endangered, as coral reefs die off, as the jellyfish invade, as the polar bears wander here and there, starving, as the soil heats up and dries out, as the lives of their own children on this earth are endangered. These corporatocrats are educated, well traveled, wealthy. As they ignore everything but the bottom line, we have to ask, for the purpose of analysis—are they primarily stupid, primarily hateful, primarily selfish, primarily power hungry, or primarily greedy?

And we have to ask ourselves, do they represent the real United States of America, destined to destroy itself because this gilded age is not like the last gilded age—the population of the world has risen from 1.7 billion in 1900 to 7.1 billion now. There is no emigrating to empty lands, no starting over, and there are many fewer resources to strip. In the late nineteenth century, at the start of the last period of serious labor unrest, American industry was known for its dangers: in 1889, the railroads employed 704,000 men, of whom 20,000 were injured and 1,972 were killed on the job. When they got hurt, it was too bad for them—there was no workers' comp, no support. Sound familiar? In the late nineteenth century, the wealthiest 2 percent of American households owned more than a third of the nation's wealth, while the top 10 percent owned roughly 75 percent. The next 50 percent had a little something, enough to be sort of middle class, and the 40 percent at the bottom had nothing. These days, it's worse. The top 1 percent owns 37 percent of everything, and the top 20 percent owns 87 percent of everything. People over sixty-five not in the 1 percent count Social Security as the largest part of their income. Paul Ryan and Donald Trump want to get rid of that.

On the night of the election, the phone rang at about 1:00 a.m. I was already asleep, but I knew it was my son. He and his friends were very worried about Trump's victory. The only comfort I could give them was that if Clinton had won, Trump's supporters would have taken to the streets, armed and violent. I still think that might have happened, and though the harassment and violence committed by Trump supporters against individuals now amounts to about a thousand incidents, they have not taken to the streets. My other children were upset, too—my stepson was crying on the way to work so that he had to pull over to the side of the road. My daughter in New York City said that everyone in her work space was crying. Only my daughter who lives in Washington, D.C., had hope—she thought Trump could be manipulated if the right people got to him first. The right people did not get to him first. You can rate Trump's cabinet picks on several scales—the is-this-guy-an-idiot scale (Ben Carson), the is-this-guy-only-in-it-for-the-money scale (Steve Mnuchin), the throw-them-to-the-dogs scale (Betsy DeVos, the person who will be glad to defund all those public schools that educated her colleagues like Tillerson and Perry), the antiabortion-gun-lover's scale (Scott Pruitt, who cares nothing about murders of the born, only of the unborn)—but they were the people who got to him first and now they have made their man—while he is working on his TV show and hanging out in Trump Tower, pondering the traffic snarl below (and, no doubt, the money he will be screwing out of the City of New York to pay for his accommodations), they will be doing in the rest of us, first by impoverishment, then by climate change.

I think I was in seventh grade when I told my mother that I wished I had been born in 1782 and died in 1860. Of course, she was aghast, but she asked why. I told her that I would have lived a long time and missed those two big wars (meaning the Revolutionary War and the Civil War), but I did not tell her why, that I was so nervous about the Cold War that I was sure it was going to happen any minute. If I had told her, she would have pooh-poohed me, and by the late '60s, I had moved on to other worries and was no longer as concerned—I decided in 1965 that maybe the Vietnam War was like a pressure valve that let off some of the U.S./ USSR steam, and we were safer than we had been.

Of course, that turned out not to be true. In the introduction of his book *War! What Is It Good For?*, Ian Morris writes about an incident that happened on my thirty-fourth birthday, September 26, 1983—at the command center of the Russians' early-warning system, the red lights went off twice, announcing a missile launch and then a missile attack on the USSR by the United States. One man, Stanislav Petrov, decided that the alert was a computer bug, even though he was terrified (Morris says that his legs gave way beneath him), and he prevented the alert from going up the chain of command, thereby averting a nuclear mistake that Morris estimates could have killed a billion people.

JFK was surrounded by generals whose ruthless embrace of winning at any cost (the cost of my life and yours) was routine. One of them was Curtis LeMay. Another, Thomas Power, said, "Restraint! Why are you so concerned with saving their lives? The whole idea is to kill the bastards! At the end of the war, if there are two Americans and one Russian, we win!" (Fred Kaplan, *The Wizards of Armageddon*). Power was commander in chief of the Strategic Air Command from 1957 to 1964. This is what he said in 1960, exactly at the time I was most terrified. Ian Morris does say that war is good for something—after lots of wars, people try peace once again (and, of course, the population is lowered, and so good times for the working class show up once again).

So what is our radical hope? One, of course, is having pure good luck, the luck that saved us from nuclear war in 1983— the good luck that placed the right person in the Russian command center, the person (and maybe there would have been others) who did not believe the evidence of his eyes but weighed it against the evidence of his instincts and made the right choice.

Another hope is that those who have been seeking power and talking more and more aggressively in order to get it might back off once the responsibility of actually having power sets in. Can they really abolish Obamacare once they have to shut their mouths and take responsibility for something? Would Thomas Power really have counted the destruction of the United States and maybe himself as an acceptable price of victory? Trump's cabinet is filled with people who have vowed to get rid of the very agencies they are in charge of. Once they know how things work, might they back off?

The third may not be so hopeful—what is the single most obvious characteristic of Trump himself? It is the desire for power and status, and the evidence that he will do anything, say anything to get it. There have been leaders like that before. But once they have power, it is never quite enough, and so they always go too far, always do themselves in. One of them, Mussolini, once he was shot, was hung upside down from a metal girder above a service station. Those whose lives he had destroyed threw stones at his corpse—the thirst for power is not a good predictor of success. Our recent voters might have seen that, but they didn't. And by the way, I do not blame the voters. It makes no sense to blame the powerless, but it does make sense to hold the powerful to account, and I think that, our fourth hope, is also our best hope—to insist on asking, over and over, "Are you human? Do you have any heart at all? Do you really believe that this nation has to be a war of all against all? Do you really believe that all men are created evil? If you don't, then act like your own power and wealth are not your first and only consideration."

When I talked to my daughter in Washington a week ago about the cabinet, she sighed and said maybe this will, finally, be the end of the baby boomers. Do you want to go out with Trump as your last representative? If not, then act!

GRACE AND KARMA UNDER ORANGE CAESAR

Luis Alberto Urrea

Midnight fools us by telling us it is dawn. That rage is righteousness. That greed is good. That women are fodder and chattel. That minorities are wicked. That the *Other* must be banned and walled out of this garden while convincing the congregation without any sense of irony that the garden is already destroyed and has been sacked and is burning. If we believe midnight, we think it's morning, and we can see clearly. But we're dreaming.

What if there is no *Other*?

What if there is only *Us*?

For a while now, I have been waiting for a leader to come direct me. A warrior to show me the way. But then it came to me: I am the warrior. So are you. We are called to lead each other through the valley.

I must share a thought before I tell you the story I have brought to this circle. It has haunted me with delight and hope, and I give it to you with pleasure. Neal Cassady once wrote to Jack Kerouac: "Grace beats Karma." Ponder that one. And add a log to the fire. I need to tell you something.

One dark era that was full of hope was the time of the civil rights movement. But that hope was under endless assault by rage and paranoia. My family lived in a barrio that was poised between warring armies of Brown and Black, with White commandos down the street. Everybody fighting for their block.

We lived in an apartment complex that was slowly being turned into Section 8 housing by absentee landlords. The battle for ownership of our street was on. And here I was, an Irish-looking Tijuana kid with a heavy Mexican accent. I accidentally offended each group of warriors. My street name could have been Target Practice.

The karma was a monster. Not only the cultural karma of what we had done to African Americans but the karma of my parents. My dad was a white Mexican, and Raza can tell you those old-school *gueros* have a special gift for bigotry. My poor mom was white, and from 1916, and she could have been written by Flannery O'Connor. She was terrified of Black faces, forbade me from having a single friend among "them." She wore a little hat and had white gloves and carried a trim little pocketbook—and she used the n-word freely. As if our neighbors wouldn't notice.

Perhaps this milieu will be illuminated by a small detail. An epiphanic detail for me. My parents put flowerpots on the steps of our concrete porch. Every step had a line of bright Mexican pots full of geraniums. To stop "them" from coming to our door. And we went in and out the back door, preferring the dirt alleyway. There could not have been a clearer racial commentary posted there if they had painted a sign. You know, like build the wall. I guess they did, come to think of it. A wall of flowers.

And late at night, someone who had simply put up with enough of white America's shenanigans and dogs and segregated drinking fountains and fire hoses came to our porch and broke every single pot. It was a slaughter of geraniums. And my parents, refusing to understand the greater text of this sad story, announced to me, "You see what they're like? That proves it." Even I knew who had been the original aggressors in this farce. And my parents rebuilt the wall with fresh pots. And those met the boot again.

Us. And Them.

Halloween wasn't a happy time for me. My mother and father were losing the chess match of their marriage, and rather than suffer through a gringo idiocy like begging neighbors for candy, my father would leave us and go bowling. And my mother would hide with the lights out lest any "colored" children came to our door. But I had reached an age when I could actually go into the street after dark. Eight!

Since we didn't have any money, my mother—who had no domestic skills—thought to make me my first costume. Depending on who suffers them, tragedies can be funny. So I liked watching Casper the Friendly Ghost, and my mother tried to make me a ghost costume. This consisted of a white sheet. And a white pillowcase with two eyeholes cut in it pulled over my head. Little Imperial Wizard. In that neighborhood. In 1963.

And out I went, no doubt parting crowds of astounded people.

The first door I stopped at was where I learned about grace. You don't know it's grace sometimes. Takes a while. But Cassady was right.

I knocked. The door opened. An older Black gentleman stood there staring at me. He took off his glasses. And he said, "What the hell are you supposed to be?"

"A ghost!"

He laughed.

"Wait a minute," he said and closed the door. He came back with his wife. And an orange. He gave me the orange.

As I left, he said, "Kid, you know what would be a lot scarier? Take off the hood. A ghost with a friendly face will really get 'em."

He saved me, knowing all about us, knowing our reputation, and seeing the walking affront to all that was holy on his porch. I took off the hood and went for more snacks. Because I didn't know any better.

There will come a time, and it won't be long, when the followers of Orange Caesar will realize that they have been lied to. That they have been fooled. That they are objects of cynical derision. And they will be hurt. We think we ache, we Nasty Women and Bad Hombres. That is when we must act. It will be our task not to gloat or mock. Because they are Us. It will be our job to comfort. We are not, in this midnight, permitted to refuse to shine.

We are the light.

Grace beats karma.

#FUCKFASCISM #FUCKTHEPATRIARCHY

Mona Eltahawy

Dear Sally,

We met tonight in Cairo when I was out grocery shopping, and you asked me if my name was Mona. You said you recognized my red hair. We spoke for just a few minutes. My beloved took a picture of the two of us, which I shall treasure, before you continued on your way with your friend and we continued our shopping.

Like me, you are of two countries—Egypt and the USA. The day we met, I was thinking of the bad guys who have been winning in both our countries. In Egypt, a military dictator has filled jails with his opponents, including young people your age, and banned protests in a bid to instill fear and obedience in a country that rose up to demand freedom and dignity in the revolution of January 25, 2011. Despite his blatant disregard for our rights, his Western allies continue to sell us out by selling him weapons, justifying it with that euphemism "solidarity."

When we met, hate was being rewarded with power and wealth in the United States.

A racist, misogynist bigot was just days away from being sworn in as U.S. president; a TV anchor who made a name for herself peddling racism had just signed a multimillion-dollar contract with a TV network; and a neo-Nazi blogger had been offered a quarter-of-a-million-dollar advance for his book.

All day long, on that day we met, I was consumed with the question: How do we make antifascism, antiracism, antimisogyny, and antibigotry rewarding and powerful? I was angry. I have been angry ever since Donald Trump was elected president. Anger fuels a lot of my work. It helps me to bulldoze my way to the words I need. All day long, as a writer, I live with words. And because I appreciate the power of words, and anger, and because I know that angry women are free women—nice and polite is how we're socialized as women, but these are not nice or polite times—I do not mince my words. So the theme of my letter to you, Sally is this: #FuckFascism and #FuckthePatriarchy. (I live on Twitter, and those two hashtags have become rallying cries for me.)

If we'd had more time on that Cairo sidewalk, I would have shared with you the ways I have determined to #FuckFascism and #FuckthePatriarchy. Instead, I came home and wrote this letter to you.

You spoke to me in Arabic; an English-accented Arabic that reminded me of my Arabic and of my younger self. Our ability to move back and forth, between countries and cultures and identities, is a tremendous privilege that enriches you in ways we need more than ever during these days of tribalism and nationalism. It can also be exhausting. Resist the demands to choose between your identities; resist the demands that you translate for one side or the other; resist the attempts by those on all the different sides of you to dilute you to one thing or to shrink you into one box.

Turn those boxes upside down! Complicate and confuse! I'm a big fan of complication—it humanizes us—and confusion—it scrambles the signals of the racists and bigots and creates space for you to be marvelous you in all your multitudes.

You are more powerful when you complicate and confuse.

I am turning fifty this year. You are turning seventeen. I wish your entrance into adulthood wasn't accompanied by such tough political times in our two countries. But I love a good fight, and I hope you do, too. In the heritage of both our countries, there are revolutionary women whose words are fuel for my revolution. I want to share some of them with you, in the hope you will find useful ammunition among them. I have learned to carry the revolution—be it against patriarchy, fascism, or bigotry—within me, so that my resistance travels with me like a beloved totem. These women's words keep that revolution—and my anger—sparkling and alive.

> *A nation cannot be liberated whether internally or*
> *externally while its women are enchained.*

> —Doria Shafik

I am first and foremost a feminist, so I begin with an Egyptian woman whose activism was central to our political rights in Egypt. In February 1951, Doria Shafik and some 1,500 women stormed the Egyptian parliament, demanding suffrage. Their action was one of the catalysts that helped gain Egyptian women the right to vote and run for political office in 1956.

I began with Shafik because I want you to remember that we have a feminist tradition in Egypt. The fight for women's equality and liberation does not belong to one nation or culture. It is global. There are women everywhere fighting patriarchy and whom I am proud to call sisters and comrades. Whether I'm fighting military rule or religious fundamentalism in Egypt, my feminism is my best weapon. Military rule and religious fundamentalism are two sides of one coin. They are both authoritarian and patriarchal. Neither of them is a friend of women's rights.

I met you, Sally, just days before the inauguration of a U.S. president who openly boasted about using his fame to grope women without their consent. Donald Trump also made racist comments against Mexicans and other Latinx people and bigoted remarks against Muslims and mocked a journalist with a disability. Trump's vice president, Mike Pence, has a long record of homophobia and enmity toward women's reproductive rights. As we prepare for the election of those two men to the highest office of the country, my feminism is once again my biggest weapon. The fight for women's equality and liberation must always target racism, bigotry, classism, ableism, and homophobia. Because as the Black lesbian poet and feminist Audre Lorde explained, *"I am not free while any woman is unfree, even when her shackles are very different from my own."*

Lorde's words, from a keynote presentation at the National Women's Studies Association Conference in 1981, are a reminder that intersectional feminism was and is the most effective way to fight patriarchy. That speech is included in *Sister Outsider: Essays and Speeches* by Audre Lorde— a book that I return to every year. In it, I find many life lessons that are vital for our fights to come.

My silences had not protected me. Your silence will not protect you.

—Audre Lorde

Patriarchy and misogyny thrive on silence. Our job in the months to come is to yell! We must shout our opposition against injustice! Silence benefits racism, misogyny, and bigotry. We must yell and shout to ensure that no one can ever use the excuse "I didn't know." As author Zora Neale Hurston put it, *"If you are silent about your pain, they'll kill you and say you enjoyed it."*

We must expose injustice. We must name and shame it. And we must stay angry because angry women are free women. Remember: fuck being nice and polite. These are not nice or polite times. Be angry. Be loud. And be free! And find your sisterhood with other angry women. Unite with them. Organize with them. Find strength with them.

The hardest and the most important revolution always has been and will continue to be in the months ahead, the revolution of the self, the revolution of the mind, and the revolution of the heart.

Revolution begins with the self, in the self. . . . We'd better take the time to fashion revolutionary selves, revolutionary lives, revolutionary relationships. . . . If your house ain't in order, you ain't in order. It is so much easier out there than right here. The revolution ain't out there. Yet. It is here.

—Toni Cade Bambara

Cherish those words from Cade Bambara's 1969 essay "On the Issue of Roles." They are touchstones that help me feel at home anywhere and everywhere because they remind me that the revolution is within me, no matter where I am. The revolution of the self is what will help you upend those boxes so many people will try to squeeze you into. That revolution of the self will help you resist demands that you choose between your identities. And that revolution of the self is what will free the multitudes you contain. Be intersectional. Make your heart too rebellious for the patriarchy's attempts to plant itself within you. Make your mind too free for fascism to chain your imagination.

And above all, as you fight patriarchy and fascism, in Egypt and in the United States, as you make yourself a mobile and transatlantic revolutionary against racism, misogyny, and bigotry, remember these words—they are my words for the revolution ahead: *resistance, stamina, sur-*

vival. The foundation for those words and the foundation of our revolution must be: *joy!*

Those of us alive and able to resist and fight mustn't capitulate to misery. What we fight for must be better.

In love, solidarity, and sisterhood,
Mona

THE FEAR AND THE RESISTANCE

Jeff Chang

We are the people, for the moment disoriented and dispossessed.

Some days we wake up and wonder what difference we can be making. We might have Solange on repeat, singing, "Be leery 'bout your place in the world / You're feeling like you're chasing the world."

She reminds us that "a king is only a man," even as he denigrates us and tries to abridge our freedom. We are weary, knowing of the fight ahead—demanding our place in the world. But as we stretch to face the day, we can also remind ourselves that we are here, and we will not go away.

In 2008, we appeared as the outline of a new majority, lifting into office a man of color who ran on twinned ideals of hope and reconciliation. Those were not to be realized, trampled in the return of the culture wars. The realpolitik of Obama's presidency all too often ran at a remove from its promise and historic meaning. But during Obama's time in office, we at least became accustomed to dignity, deliberation, and some measure of honesty. And through our people power, we pushed the presidency to important breakthroughs.

Now we are in the grip of Trump and his disturbing pathologies: his aversion to truth or reflection; his imperious, inescapable self-aggrandizement; his casual embrace of violence and brutality; his insistence that we do not belong in this nation's future.

This presidential election was triply devastating. The country was left more divided than at any time since the Civil War. The expression of a new majority—both numerical and cultural—was denied. And the forces of reaction were given back unchecked control of the nation. When Trump began appointing the looters, warmongers, conspiracists, resegregationists, and other assorted arsonists who make up his cabinet, some of us objected, saying, "This is not normal." But presidencies are not simply matters of personal style. In a nation built by the many for the few, under genocide, forced labor, exclusion, misogyny, imperialism, and segregation, Trump has behaved as most presidents have, perhaps only with less restraint.

Yet the election also reminds us of the revolutionary roots of our country. We hear the enduring moral call: governments "derive their just powers from the consent of the governed." We deny our consent when we say, "He is not my president." Although we must live for now with the compromises the founders made that continue to thwart direct democracy, we are not required to find faith with an unrepresentative minority. We place our faith in the power of the real majority and a future still waiting to be written.

Undoubtedly, Trump represents the restoration of whiteness. In 2008, at the end of the Bush II regime and the start of the Great Recession, a psychological bubble was burst. English pop star Lily Allen captured the transatlantic moment in her song "The Fear."

Urged on by leaders who promise a no-fault war and prescribe consumer therapy for its traumas, Lily's character has become "a weapon of mass consumption." Credit cards are her assault rifles. She rhymes "packing plastic" with descriptions of a life "so fuckin' fantastic." She is winning the game. But she is aware that the bill is coming due, that she is hurtling into the void.

"I don't know what's right or what's real anymore / I don't know how I'm meant to feel anymore," she sings. "When do you think it will all become clear / And I'll be taken over by the fear?"

Politics is now engaged in the business of orchestrating, exacerbating, and managing the fears created by speed and technology. Paul Virilio calls this shift "the administration of fear"—a phrase we might take on multiple levels. "Fear," he says, "is now an environment, a surrounding, a world." It is encompassing, enclosing, and self-replicating. One fear intensifies another and on and on in an interminable set of loops. Spectacular events further "synchronize emotion on a global scale" and advance the "transition from a democracy of opinion to a democracy of emotion."

Trump's rise is due in no small part to his administration of fear from his own phone. To those trapped in this environment, who are unable to imagine any other reality, even Trump's most unhinged tweets must feel like life preservers. By now it is also clear that Farage and his Brexiters knew exactly what to tell Lily Allen's bereft character she was meant to feel. Fear is the lubricant of demagoguery, and what demagogues best understand is that all anxieties flow back to the fear of the Other.

Here's where Trump's unusual position at the juncture of pop and politics served him well. One of the founding archetypes of American pop culture is the narrative of the impending white racial apocalypse. Trump's hair-metal rallies and Twitter rants have their roots in Buffalo Bill Cody's Wild West show and D. W. Griffith's 1915 film *The Birth of a Nation*—stories of deliverance from the barbarism of natives and former slaves. A half century after *The Birth of a Nation*, Richard Nixon summoned the apocalypse against the civil rights and antiwar movements with two words—*crime* and *disorder*. Trump's earliest campaign placards read, THE SILENT MAJORITY STANDS WITH TRUMP. But he could not duplicate Nixon's call with facts. Crime was at historically low rates, and, since the Great Recession, net migration from Mexico had dropped below zero. He won most of his electoral votes in places far from the border and urban strife, places clouded by the ambience of distant fear. He won on affect, not facts.

White anxiety is as complicated as it is toxic. It consists of an emotional miasma in which real economic woes conjoin with existential dolor, seen in tragically rising rates of opioid addiction and suicide. A sense of demographic and cultural decline figure here, too. Obama evoked powerful and contradictory emotions. His presence alone provoked primal rages. But as the embodiment of excellence and achievement, he also confirmed the myths of American meritocracy. And so he also ignited white fears of falling, anxieties rooted in meritocracy's zero-sum logic, wherein a gain for communities of color signals a loss for whites.

The worry of the exurban futures trader is not the precarity of the Appalachian carpenter. Trump needed a frame that would capture them all. As he began courting the angry outsider groups sprung up in the sidewalk cracks of the far right—Birthers, Tea Party activists, white nationalists, Breitbart.com readers—he found his restorationist message. Trump offered a kind of vulgar Reaganism shorn of humor, ideology, and sentimentality, and always delivered in the first-person singular. Strength. Walls. Greatness. Those sources of disorder—the Blacks, the Mexicans, the Muslims, the women? "I am your voice," he said. "I alone can fix it."

It is impossible to overestimate the power of the Fear. It overwhelms facts, tolerates the rankest misogyny, countenances stunning mediocrity, and is unafraid to reveal its immorality. As Michael Flynn, later the short-lived National Security Advisor, in a doublespeak as banal as it is evil, once tweeted, "Fear of Muslims is rational: please forward this to others: the truth fears no questions."

Racism is the fear that Virilio describes—"a collective madness" unable to withstand the lightest of interrogation. But its endurance is due to the fact that it is also a system that produces material rewards for the few. Trump deployed it to support himself and a specific subclass of wealthy white men who have made their fortunes through pillaging, displacement, exclusion, and inheritance. Every day in office, Trump will reveal the point of his kleptocracy—to continue to accumulate as much as he can.

And so here we are, the real majority, learning to live (again) without illusion. That means, above all, conquering the Fear and expressing new desires for a new nation and world.

In the fevered days of his first presidential primary campaign, Obama famously delivered a line popularized by Alice Walker, first written by June Jordan: "We are the ones we've been waiting for." It became a favorite epigram of those mobilizing to deliver the presidency. That year, our forces for change narrowed into an all-or-nothing gambit at the polls. But when that bet paid off, we had shockingly little local infrastructure to further our agenda. A racist backlash filled the breach.

By his second term, our justice movements—decades-old efforts to transform the social imagination and open paths for change—had pushed the Obama administration toward many of its most powerful breakthroughs.

Marriage equality—which Obama opposed as a candidate—succeeded because artists and activists had transformed the way LGBTQ people were seen. Obama's move to bring undocumented youths out of the shadows with an executive order allowing them to defer deportation and receive work permits occurred only after DREAMers and immigrant rights artists and activists had humanized the stories of undocumented families and shamed the administration for its historic levels of deportations. The Occupy movement introduced the language of the "99 percent" and reset the terms around discussion of inequality for the next two presidential elections.

And the Black Lives Matter movement changed it all,

refocusing our efforts to understand inequality from the most important gap—life expectancy between Blacks and whites. The movement has reinvigorated national discussions about policing, militarization, and mass incarceration, but also school and housing resegregation, campus diversity, and cultural equity.

We understand that class is inseparable from race, gender, and sexuality—that power comes from exposing and understanding the intersectionalities. Unfortunately, this lesson seems to have been lost on restorationists who claim to be progressive but have also been taken over by the Fear.

In a moment when politics feels hopelessly deadlocked and closed, the Movement for Black Lives has ushered in a kind of cultural renaissance, prompting artists, organizers, and thinkers to explore an efflorescence of new social visions—modes, metaphors, and processes of justice making and community building. We know that cultural change precedes political change. What we also know is that it will always be our special burden to explore and advance new imaginations that arouse desires for change.

In a country haunted by injustice and inequality, the weight of history is always set against us. All that the forces of reaction must do is appropriate our visions and language to reinforce the status quo. Our constant struggle is to overcome that stasis, and that requires us to move, seduce, and inspire people to manifest ideas of a nation and a world still yet to be, to—as Toni Cade Bambara once put it—make the revolution irresistible.

Over the past several years, as we have manifested our freedom dreams into material demands, we have built infrastructures that have us more prepared than we might think. We find ourselves in a moment that is different from other postpresidential election moments: justice movements are activated and on high alert. Trump's presidency will mobilize our opposition the way that the symbol of Obama consolidated the fringes of the right. But where they fostered hatred and distrust, we welcome those who will do the work. Where they shut the doors and locked them, we will fling them open. Our first person is always plural.

We are a possible coalition of the willing: feminists fighting for reproductive justice, indigenous people protecting water, environmentalists holding strong on climate change agreements, Muslims standing for civil rights, African Americans pushing against policing and mass incarceration, Latinos and Asian Americans demanding immigration reform, all of us opposing economic turbulence, reactionary jurisprudence, and kleptocratic governance, all of us pressing for freedom for all.

As we face the new day, we must remind ourselves: We are not alone. We are not marginal. We are the majority. We are ready. And we will not stay silent.

Seeds

A LETTER TO MY DAUGHTER

Claire Messud

Dear Livia,

When you were seven weeks old, we took you to a wedding in New York City. We dressed you in an embroidered white linen dress I'd also worn as an infant, we combed what little hair you had, we popped you in the car seat and zoomed down from western Massachusetts. With the exception of the lovely bride, you were the belle of the ball—handed from aspiring grandmother to aspiring grandmother, chin-chucked, dandled, cooed over, cuddled. Daddy surreptitiously changed your diaper in the library of the fancy private club. A television star praised your dimples. You loved every minute and didn't cry once.

Two days later, less than twenty-four hours after we got home, al-Qaeda terrorists hijacked passenger jets and flew them into a field in rural Pennsylvania, the Pentagon, and the Twin Towers, killing thousands. The world into which we thought you had been born was ineradicably altered in a matter of hours. So began the terrible Time of Fear, the better part of a decade in which our actions and reactions as a nation were premised on constant dread and anxiety. We prosecuted wars on false pretenses; we blithely dispensed with our fundamental moral beliefs and turned a blind eye to extraordinary rendition and torture. With arrogant ignorance, inadequate military preparations, and botched strategies, we sacrificed countless young men and women, both on the battlefield and afterward, many of them victims of severe injuries whose lives can never be fully restored. We treated our allies in the region with cavalier indifference (remember Kirk Johnson, Daddy's friend from Berlin, who started the List Project and worked so hard to help Iraqis abandoned by the American government for whom they'd worked?). In the course of these years, we alienated a generation of young people across the Middle East. When I visited Turkey in 2007 as a cultural guest of the State Department, it was explained to me that under Bill Clinton, the United States had had a more than 75 percent approval rating in Turkey. By the last years of George W. Bush's presidency, that rating was 9 percent. And 50 percent of the Turkish population was under twenty-five years old, which meant that most young Turks had never thought well of our country.

In 2008, Barack Obama ran for president with the slogan "Yes We Can," on a platform of "Hope." You turned seven years old that year—the age of reason—and both at home and in the country, the optimism was palpable. Your friend Annie favored Hillary and dressed up as HRC for Halloween; you liked them both, Hillary and Obama, and didn't mind who won. Even though you were still small, you laughed at Sarah Palin jokes—not realizing, I think, that they were funny only because she wasn't elected.

We believed that we could, as a nation, surmount our fear together. We believed in choosing peaceful dialogue instead of conflict, in openness and tolerance instead of division and hatred. We believed in a progressive future instead of a return to the past. These past eight years have not been without problems or limitations. But it has a been a gift for you—and for us, raising you—to grow to maturity in a political culture that supports equal rights, dignity, and mutual respect for all, that believes in global cooperation on important issues as diverse as climate change and world peace.

Now, my daughter, you're approaching sixteen. This year, you were passionate about the election: first about Bernie Sanders, then about Hillary Clinton. Passionate, too, about the unfortunate alternative, the man who will now be our president: passionate about the many ways in which his vision for America is diametrically opposed to yours, passionate about how dire the consequences of his policies will be—for the truth, for facts, for the rule of law, for dignity, for women, for minorities, for the environment, for workers, for world peace.

Here we go again, back into a permanent defensive crouch, a return to the Time of Fear we knew when you were a little girl. It's not that we can't get through this—of course we can. As Katharine Viner, the editor of *The Guardian*, wrote to subscribers on November 9, the day after the election, "Progressive ideas are good ideas and *The Guardian* will never turn away from them." Nor should any of us. I know you won't. But I'm sorry that you're launched so young into the fight: I would have wished for a few more years of relatively straightforward optimism. I know you're at the ready, too. I know you and your peers have the faith, the patience, and the fortitude that will be demanded of you.

Remember that this man is not the cause of our society's problems; he is merely the symptom. If we battle those ills, we can defeat him. He is the face of many of our failings, his rise the confluence of diverse problems to which we have failed, as a nation, to attend. With the disappearance of any counterbalancing Marxist—or even socialist—discourse, Americans have become utterly enslaved to mammon. (Bernie Sanders and his followers represent the national outrage at this situation.) Like some parody from central casting, the Demagogue in Chief believes his wealth alone entitles him to the highest office in the land; and apparently, many voters, too, have lost sight of the fact that statesmanship is not the same as business acumen. Our national moral compass is wildly askew: as long ago as 2009, in the wake of the financial crash, I listened to a commentator on NPR explain that the rights of the individual had been enshrined in the Constitution precisely because they had been previously considered supernumerary. It never occurred to the Founding Fathers that the rights of the individual could threaten the common good; and yet, the commentator lamented, by 2009, this was the pass to which our society had come. In the 1980s, 1,100 people were prosecuted after the savings and loan crisis; in the wake of the 2008 financial crisis, only one top banker went to jail. This was the result of a shift in mores over those twenty years: Americans, obsessed with personal gain, no longer see the common good as the highest good. Indeed, the unnameable-elect, in debate, could argue that his failure to pay taxes—an abdication of which millionaires of yore would rightly have been ashamed—was simply a matter of his intelligent use of a legal loophole. In other words, his scrupulous attention to his private wealth was a matter for public admiration rather than condemnation. And he was elected for it.

Then, too, there's our social media problem, and its concomitant—though preexisting—celebrity problem. We've talked a lot, latterly, about fake news, and that's certainly an issue. But the Gordian knot has many strands. We're ever more powerfully grafted to our devices and are hence always immersed in the general cacophony of contemporary existence, inundated by noise and information so that it becomes impossible to tell vital details from fripperies, seriousness from nonsense. We used to know that the *National Enquirer* was not *The New York Times*; with the advent of the *Daily Mail* online, the distinctions are no longer so clear. Another strand is our willful infantilization as a culture: we seek constant distraction, amusement, and simplification; and purveyors of information (and so-called news) are only too happy to oblige. Syntactically, analytically, conceptually—we grow ever lazier, and alas, before long the 140-character tweet will come to represent the length of our attention spans. You and your peers will have to take responsibility for this world of idiocy that my generation has foisted upon you, and will have to demand, of yourselves, a greater commitment to and engagement with complex realities. Some truths are irreducible. Important matters require effort and patience, and can often be boring as well as arduous. Life is no bowl of cherries; nor is it a Doodle Fruit Game.

Then, too, there is our society's disingenuous myth-making, the lies we tell ourselves to dull rebellion. The American dream, as Ta-Nehisi Coates has recently observed, remains for many (particularly minorities) a false promise. You remember the obese, unwell, and aging taxi driver who routinely took us to the airport before dawn, obsessively ranting against Obamacare, because when he makes his millions he doesn't want to have to pay for anyone else's medical bills? He's one of many deluded by a fantasy, a fantasy that Donald Trump has rekindled and encouraged: the idea that each of us is a millionaire in waiting, who should behave with all the superiority and scorn of a millionaire, in the firm belief that the individual matters more than society, and in the firm belief that money matters more than background (which it may) or than education (which it may not) or than morals (which it cannot), and that money will soon be ours.

Remember our amazing evening at *King Lear*? Can you see, in your memory, Lear mad upon the heath, besmirched in his tattered loincloth, his crown of weeds, his kingdom and his power lost? We joked afterward that the new president should be made to sit through it, and you laughingly said he wouldn't, he couldn't. Because the play's lessons—its wise truths—were too uncomfortable for such a man to endure. "Handy-dandy, which is the justice, which is the thief? . . . A dog's obeyed in office. . . . Robes and furred gowns hide all. Plate sin with gold / And the strong lance of justice hurtless breaks." Only when he wanders naked and abandoned in the storm does Lear realize, at last, that all men are the same; that the greatest and least among us are kin. That there but for the grace of God, and so forth.

It's a lesson all of us must learn, sooner or later. For many, it isn't until we're near death. You were too young to remember it, but I truly understood it first when Grandpa was in the rehab hospital, the first time he was dying, not in his right mind (though mercifully his wits eventually came back), around the time he waved a twirling finger in the air—not unlike Lear, in fact—and said, "I know what this is—it's a fiesta!" And a nurse's aide came in, her shoes squeaking on the linoleum, clipboard in hand, and asked, in efficient tones, without looking at the man in the bed, "What was he, before?" Suddenly I grasped, truly, that my father, whom I so loved and had so feared, had held in awe, was, too, no more than a poor, bare, forked animal— unaccommodated man—the same as anyone else. I would learn it again and again, in the course of my parents' illnesses, their respective journeys to the grave. All that we believe defines us counts for nothing. Ultimately, each of us is not just Lear in his (lucid) madness; we're Poor Tom himself.

As Tom knows: "Yet better thus, and known to be contemned, / Than still contemned and flattered. To be worst, / The lowest and most dejected thing of fortune / Stands still in esperance, lives not in fear. / The lamentable change is from the best; / The worst returns to laughter. Welcome, then, / Thou unsubstantial air that I embrace! / The wretch that thou hast blown unto the worst / Owes nothing to thy blasts."

To live in hope, without fear, with nothing to lose: that's

freedom. And that's what democracy should allow. Any society that believes that money is the greatest power can't truly be free. The wise have always known it—from Jesus Christ to Julian of Norwich (the medieval mystic whose adage is my mantra: "All shall be well, and all shall be well, and all manner of thing shall be well") to Shakespeare to Gandhi, Mandela, and perhaps even Obama. This callow soul our nation has recently elected to its highest office is far from attaining this fundamental knowledge; as, one must presume, are too many of our fellow citizens.

But that's not a reason to pretend we don't know the truth. And knowing it, we must choose to live differently: in the understanding that the refugee, the outcast, the other, the criminal, they're Poor Tom also—we're all the same, naked on the blasted heath. As James Lowell wrote in the *Boston Courier* in 1845, in what would become one of the oft-sung hymns of my childhood, "Once to every man and nation, comes the moment to decide." The poem's last verse reads (or sings) thus: "Though the cause of evil prosper, yet the truth alone is strong; / Though her portion be the scaffold, and upon the throne be wrong; / Yet that scaffold sways the future, and behind the dim unknown, / Standeth God within the shadow, keeping watch above His own."

I'm not religious in any traditional sense, and nor are you (or not just now). But the moral imperative remains as clear for us as it does for any devout believer. We know in our bones that there is right, and there is wrong; and we know that in difficult times as much as in the easy ones, we must defend what we believe to be right. "Though her portion be the scaffold"—we hope, in this nation in this time, that things won't come to that. But we can't be sure; and to quote again from the wise William Shakespeare—though Hamlet, this time—"The readiness is all."

You were born into strife, or all but. You're so young, still, and as I say, I'd wish for you that the struggles presented by this presidency and its follies didn't loom so clearly and alarmingly before you. But alas, dear one, we can't ignore the call: our futures—not just ours personally but those of the nation and the world we love—depend upon it. As Poor Tom knew, as Lear came to know, we're all bare human beings beneath our clothes, humble in our lives and deaths. Power and prominence are as meaningless as wealth and beauty. All is vanity. This hollow president—vanity incarnate—is the voice of a hollow culture; hollow men (and women, Kellyanne Conway!) are abroad in the land.

So, Livia, my dearest daughter, it's up to us—and in the future, it will be up to you—to defend substance, to forge a true path, and a meaningful one. To be fearless, joyful, hopeful. Privileged as we are, we have an obligation to be happy, to work for justice, openness, and generosity whenever possible; to listen fully to complexities and to try our best to understand; to hold the lamp illumined and aloft. No good gesture is wasted. No kindness is otiose. No sacrifice is too great. Each of us must shed light wherever we can.

Courage, my love. I have great faith in you, and in your generation. I'm always at your side, holding your hand. We're stronger together.

Your mum

THE MOST IMPORTANT ACT OF RESISTANCE

Meredith Russo

Darwin,

I expect you won't read this until you're much older. You're only two now, a beautiful little toddler who I am told looks just like me; whether the comparison is an insult or a compliment will be up to you, I suppose. When you do read this, and when you realize how many people have already read it, you might be embarrassed at the things your mother has shared, or you might be proud. Again, time will have to tell, because I certainly can't. I remember when I thought I could predict what the future held, at least in a general sense, but now? At the end of the year 2016, or 5776 in the faith of your birth, as hate rises like a tide around the world, that thought seems like arrogance, and it has been replaced by fear.

I am familiar with fear. I felt it the night you were conceived, when I took my first dose of hormone therapy, my first step to aligning my body with my mind. I realized I might never have another shot at a child of my own and decided to give you one chance to show me you were meant to be. I felt it when you were born, and I held your tiny, fragile body and thought of what life might have in store for you. I feel it for you every day when I read about synagogues burned and defaced all over America, about Jews demeaned in code and then in the open, about people saying you should be taken from me because being raised by someone like me is abuse, when I look in your eyes and only see trust and love. We face an oncoming storm, my sweet child, a thunderhead that gives pause even to those accustomed to oppression, indignity, and brutality, and I am not ashamed to admit I am more afraid than ever. I pray that it ends soon, that sanity prevails and we right our course before too many of history's mistakes are repeated—but people are imperfect, and I have never really believed in prayer So I must grapple with the reality that you will in all likelihood grow up in the rain, the shadow, and the thunder. You will become an adult in a world tainted by fear, and for that I am sorry.

Listen to me when I tell you what fear is capable of: it can keep you safe, and it can mangle your soul. Your countrymen let the powerful twist their fear until they believed that women like me, and Jews like you, and people of color and Muslims and immigrants were threats and barely human beings at all. I know this from experience as well. When I was young, I feared my body's inevitable betrayal as it tried to turn me into a man. I feared shame and ridicule, feared abandonment by friends and family, feared bullying, and feared the threats of violence, degradation, and rape that I knew came with life as a woman. I let my fear twist me into a person I look back on with shame, a young "man" who alienated friends, resented peers, insulted family, lashed out at others before they could strike first, and acted tone deaf to the needs of others. That I was already beaten and mocked for seeming "gay" when I was young was the proof I needed that I was right. I wasted twenty-six years on lonely, terrible, bitter fear. I tried killing myself to escape it, but, since that didn't work, I faced it.

I became the woman I had always needed to be or, rather, ceased pretending to be a man. And you know what? My fears all came true.

It was too late to undo what years of testosterone had done, it became almost impossible to find work, I lost family members and strained relations with others, total strangers went out of their way to vomit hate into my various in-boxes, I was beaten, I was catcalled, and, yes, I was sexually assaulted. But despite what my fear had insisted, none of it, not even that last bit, was the end of the world. In fact, quite the opposite: since transitioning, I have grown closer with the family that matters than I ever was before, I have snagged the job of my dreams, I have strengthened the friendships I already had and formed new ones I could not have imagined before, I have danced and loved in a body that felt closer to whole than I thought possible, I have helped women and girls like me, and, most important of all, I have received the honor of being your mother. Had I let fear continue to mutilate me, none of this would have happened, and you alone are worth everything I have endured. Always remember that there are things in your life worth enduring infinite agony for, and that it is in the best interest of the hateful to keep them from you through fear.

You are the Jewish child of a queer transgender woman. You have queerness in your genes, to the extent that it might be genetic. Life would have been hard for you before these clouds formed, but now . . . well. I had hoped to hand you a kinder, gentler world than the one I grew up in, one where the suffering and shame I endured in my youth would seem like a relic of history, but my hope was misplaced. Nationalism, racism, xenophobia, homophobia, misogyny, and anti-Semitism are in their ascendancy, and they will not recede again without raking their claws through the world as they go. We will be targets. This is inevitable, and it is horrifying, especially as a parent, but we must not let it rule us. Every moment our fears and anxieties hold dominion over us is a moment that those who hate have stolen from us, and we must give them nothing. Look at my life whenever you doubt this. Look at yourself, and remember that I would not have you if I had given in. I will protect you as much as I can for as long as I can, but as you grow into yourself, as you finally read this, please promise me that you will, insofar as any person can, set your fear aside and devote yourself to a full, honest life. That, my child, is the first and most important act of resistance any of us can undertake.

Love,
MerMer

TO MY GODDAUGHTER

Reyna Grande

DECEMBER 22, 2016

My dearest Reynita,

Little one, my goddaughter, my namesake, when you were in your mother's womb, I wondered if there would be anything I could do to shelter you from what awaits you living in a place like Iguala, Guerrero, Mexico. I worry even more now that you are here with us. I was deeply honored when your mother, my cousin Diana, asked me to be your godmother. At four weeks old, you were the littlest baby in the Iglesia de las Maravillas, the Church of Miracles. We all felt a certain urgency to have you blessed and protected in these uncertain times. In a month, the country I've called home for more than thirty years will have a new leader, someone who cares nothing about you or me. Even before you were conceived, this man launched his campaign for president of the United States by calling Mexican immigrants "rapists, criminals, and drug dealers." He insulted all the family you have in the United States—your uncle Ángel (whom your mother hasn't seen in ten years) and my siblings and me. He said that Mexico doesn't send its best, and yet we have given the very best of ourselves: our work ethic, our skills, our talents, our passion.

In your life, you will learn that everything that happens in the United States affects Mexico, usually for the worse. Two weeks before you were born, the Mexican peso dropped in value more than it had in twenty years the day after Donald Trump was declared our next president! He sealed his election by promising to build a wall between our countries and deport the eleven million undocumented immigrants living in the United States, including your uncle. When your mother was a baby, the U.S. president at the time began to build a wall. How is it that now that *you* are a baby, more walls are being built? I want to give you a world without divisions, with no borders. Beyond the bricks and the barbed wires, I wish I could remove the barriers that will hinder your growth, kill your spark, rob you of your potential, deny you all that you deserve. I tried to save your mother but was unable to, and as I held you in my arms at your baptism, I prayed to be allowed to do for you what I couldn't do for her.

When I met your mother, she was a year old. It was my first visit back to Mexico since I'd immigrated to the United States. I was seventeen, more American than Mexican by then. Eight years in the States had done that to me— stripped me of my identity so that I no longer knew who I was: not Mexican enough in Mexico, but also not American enough in the States. It had robbed me of my native tongue so that it felt foreign in my mouth. On that visit to Mexico,

I was struggling with more than my clumsy Spanish. I was struggling with the reality of our family's life in Iguala. For the first time, I was seeing our hometown through different eyes—American eyes. The poverty in which your mother lived astounded me, though it was the same poverty I'd been born into. I had tried to forget that I was born in a shack of sticks and cardboard, just like the place where your mother now lived. I'd tried to forget the dirt roads of Iguala, the trash heaps burning along the train tracks, the bare-foot children with swollen bellies full of tapeworms and heads infested with lice, the way my bare feet burned on the scalding road on the way to the tortilla mill, the horse dung floating by me as I bathed in the canal, the way my palms blistered from the buckets of water I carried home from the community well.

I had tried to forget, and I had succeeded, because in Los Angeles, I lived in relative comfort; my childhood in Mexico faded away, like a nightmare best forgotten. And you might not believe this, but by American standards, my family lived in poverty in LA. Yet coming from Mexico—knowing what real poverty feels like, looks like, smells like—made me feel rich. My father, a maintenance worker with a third-grade education, could not afford to give us much, but our house had walls made of drywall and stucco, a shingled roof, a carpeted floor, running water, and electricity—luxuries we never had in Mexico. So, in shock I looked at that shack where your mother lived with its corrugated metal roof, with sticks tied with rope for walls, a dirt floor, a toilet that didn't flush from lack of running water.

When I returned to LA, I brought your mother with me

in my mind and in my heart. Little one, I felt guilty that I could leave, that I had that option, that I could get on an airplane and fall asleep, then wake up in a place your mother could only dream about. I wondered what Mexico would offer her and her future children—you! I wondered what kind of life you would all have. It made me think of the choices our parents had made and the impact they'd had on us. Your grandparents chose to stay in Mexico and make do with what little the country had to offer them. They learned not to ask for anything from their government. My own parents chose a different path—to leave Mexico and seek a better life in the United States. My father paid a smuggler and took his three children across the border, risking our lives, yes, for a shot at the American Dream. There was heartbreak and sorrow, I'll tell you that, and challenges as we struggled to learn English, adjust to a new way of life, live in the shadows. To our dismay, there were many barriers to overcome even after we crossed the U.S. border: language barriers, cultural barriers, legal barriers, and more. Life in the States isn't like the stories you'll hear back in Mexico. It isn't a fairy tale with a happy ending. Not completely. This society is good at putting up barriers for its immigrant population, especially the undesirables—people of color. To survive, to have a chance at the American Dream, we must learn to dream fully awake, our eyes wide open. We see the grim side of the fairy tale. We learn to persevere, to ignore the wolf breathing down our necks.

As time passed, I worried about your mother. She wasn't taught how to dream, little one, as I was. I returned to see her through the years, fell in love with her again and again—her laughter, her innocence, the way she followed me around to make each minute count. She was fascinated by the cousin who lived in America, in that special place everyone longed for. She thought I lived in Disneyland! I left a little piece of my heart in Iguala, with her. I worried when I heard that, at thirteen, she had dropped out of middle school to go work at a maquila, a garment factory owned by a U.S. corporation, getting paid a measly five dollars a day, working six days a week and overtime. She became part of that "cheap labor" that Mexico seems so proud to be able to offer U.S. companies. I didn't judge her. I knew she did it to help your grandmother. But even when I offered to send money so she could return to school, she refused. Perhaps she already knew that where you live, education isn't much of an investment. I worried about her when I heard that, at sixteen, she'd gotten pregnant with your older sister. But she has found a good man in your father, one who has been there by her side.

I also worried when I saw how America's addiction to drugs had impacted Mexico—our state of Guerrero became the biggest supplier of heroin, the beautiful mountains that surround our hometown were suddenly covered in poppy fields, our local bus station now doubled as a distribution center for the cartel. Afraid for your mother when, in September 2014, forty-three college students were disappeared in our hometown by the police, a mere ten minutes from where you live. I came to Iguala and begged her to let me pay for her schooling. I wanted to give your mother an education so that she could have options in a place where options are few. I wanted her to have a chance for success living in a city where even the mayor is complicit in the crimes the cartel commits, where on a regular basis mass graves are discovered a few kilometers from your home, where human rights mean nothing. Naïvely, I thought I could give her a way out without having to leave Mexico, as I did. I never encouraged her to immigrate, to pay a smuggler to bring her. No, I didn't want to risk your mother's life, your father's, your sister's. I didn't want to subject them to the hardships that undocumented immigrants face in the United States, especially in these bleak times when anti-immigrant sentiments are being fueled by fear and ignorance. I didn't want your sweet mother to live in the shadows of U.S. society, as I did once.

She accepted my offer to pay for her to go to school, but I was wrong. I had let my American mentality, my American Dream, get in the way. Two years later, with her schooling behind her at the local beauty school—after the thousands of pesos in tuition, in materials, in equipment—the best Iguala can offer your mother is 80 pesos a day for working as an *estilista*, a beautician. In a place where a pizza costs 200 pesos, that daily salary is a slap in the face.

This morning, I left Iguala to return to my home in California, and little one, I confess that in the twenty-three years I've come and gone, I've learned to say good-bye to your mother and deal with the ache of our bittersweet separation. But today, it was excruciating to have to say good-bye to you. Leaving you in Iguala—the way I've left your mother—means you will grow up as your parents have done, resigned to living in a country full of corruption and greed. You will always know that no government official is to be trusted. That everything that comes out of the mayor's, governor's, the president's mouth is a lie. That he will sell your city, your state, your country to the highest bidder to fatten his pockets, just like Mexican officials in power have always done. You will learn to accept that the United States and Mexico are, and will continue to be, in bed together regardless of who the presidents are, because politics is a dirty business, and it all comes down to money and power. You will come to the bitter realization that neither country has your best interests at heart. That whatever policies they implement, whatever trade agreements they sign, whatever joint ventures they cook up together, whatever U.S.-owned factories open in your town, they are not to keep you safe, not to improve your life, not to bring you better opportunities, not to give you a decent livelihood. You will grow up expecting nothing from your government and even less from mine, especially with this new leader. You will learn to accept your situation. You will learn to keep your head down and your mouth shut. You will learn to ignore being miserable.

Today I wished I could take you with me. I wished I could find a way to defy everyone and everything that keeps me from doing so. But how could I turn you into an immigrant, especially now when I don't know what kind of challenges this new president will bring us? If you stay in Mexico, you'll never have to be an unwanted stranger in a new land. You'll never have to question your identity. You'll always be as Mexican as everyone around you. For better or worse, you will always belong to your country and it to you. You will never have to give up your native tongue or cultural roots. You will never be "othered." You will never be accused of being a criminal. You will never be made to feel that you are not enough. The only thing against you is that you are poor. And though poverty brings many heartaches and sorrows, the stigma of being an immigrant, especially at times like now, isn't what I want for you.

Wherever you are, what I want for you is what I've managed to have—an education, a successful career, a good home, a life lived to the fullest. To be honest, I don't know the best way to give you all this. The obstacles before us sometimes seem insurmountable. But I promise to be there for you, always, and to give you all that I can give. I promise you sanctuary whenever you need it. I promise to share my dreams with you and to nourish the dreams you share with me. Now more than any other time, despite the border between us, our family needs to be there for each other, to look out for each other, to fight for each other, because one thing that is certain is this: during Trump's presidency, those who stand to lose the most are the ones who have the least—and that includes our family, little one.

Your mother once thought I lived in Disneyland, and I do live in a magical place. Despite the racism and hatred that at times rear their ugly heads, like now, there is also much kindness and generosity here. There are people who care about and respect each other regardless of where they come from. I return to the States now more determined than ever to fight to keep this country a place that is compassionate and generous to all human beings. As your godmother, I am more determined to push for bridges, not walls, to be built between the United States and Mexico and to improve life in both places by continuing to give my best. Through my books and my public speaking, my activism and advocacy, I'm fighting for you and me to have a country where dreams exist, where everything is possible if we work hard enough, where we honor our commonalities and respect our differences, where we celebrate what makes us unique. I will continue to fight to make both our countries places where democracy is strong, social mobility is possible, and people live in harmony. Little one, I promise you I will fight to give you the life that you deserve.

With love and light,
Your godmother

LANGUAGE IS HOW YOU WILL MAKE YOURSELF

Katie Kitamura

Dear Mila,

In the days after the election, there is a torrent of language around me—on the Internet, the radio, the news, the social media streams of the president-elect—but it fails to bring the world into being. I listen, and I read, and I listen, and still I cannot comprehend the world that is being described. I hold you in my lap, and I say to your father, "What are they saying? What do they mean?" He shakes his head and doesn't answer.

For the first time in my life, I'm unable to read fiction. I dedicate my days to the news, which is constantly breaking over all our heads. I read it while I nurse you, while you are sleeping. I spend my time absorbing what is being referred to as the new reality, one that has immediate and material effect but continues to feel like a simulation, too thin to be real.

I'm aware that this disbelief is a luxury, and it makes me feel slow and stupid. Because of you, I want more than anything to be practical, to act with efficiency. Instead, I find myself staring at a world that seems completely depthless. No matter how much I read, the language feels unsteady, as if it, too, has capitulated in this age of post-truth. The very phrase *post-truth* is a sign of this capitulation.

The president-elect's abuse of language is something your father and I laughed about, while I was pregnant with you. But the language he uses, its syntactical collapse, no longer seems comically inept, but sly and calculated. The weaker the common language, the harder it is to understand the true consequences of what is happening, of what is being dismantled and what is being erected in its place.

The effect is immediate. In the days after the election, words break apart in my mouth. I call my congressman, only to be put on hold for half an hour, only to find my voice hesitant and trembling when I am finally put through. I stumble over my words, my speech is as senseless as that of the president-elect, a realization that fills me with horror. The woman at the other end of the line is patient, and when I finally fall silent, she tells me that they have received many similar calls and that they are taking a tally so the numbers can be communicated to the congressman.

She is kind, but I notice that it is numbers rather than words, and I know that the words I did manage to speak did not have sufficient force. Other are writing to better effect, in essays and in Facebook posts, in e-mails and in articles—against the torrent of language that flows out of the president-elect's mouth, they reply with their own tide of words. Although I want to contribute to this chorus of voices, although I want to be one of this new plurality, I find that I am still paralyzed.

I can't find my words. I try to do other things. I donate, I attend protests, I call. I use the words of other people: at one point, I find a script online to help when I call my representatives. But I start to suspect that I am bad at thinking in real time, bad at speaking out. I remember my own mother, who moved to this country without any English and who was silenced into silencing herself, who would jump with fright every time the telephone rang or hide in the closet rather than answer the door.

In this moment, I, too, lack confidence in the words at my disposal. I need a language adequate to this impossible world, one that will help me act upon it. But language is malleable, and it is not always on the side of truth. This is something every writer knows. Words make and unmake the world with terrifying rapidity, and they do so without moral distinction. It is happening now, in the executive orders being drafted, in the epithets denigrating minorities and women, in the conflicts spawned in bursts of 140 characters. The man who refuses to be accountable to his own words now wields language with the authority of a tyrant.

There is a battle going on right now over the words we use, over who has the right to speak and who does not. And so, in the same way that my mother forced herself to learn English in order to fight for her children, I force myself to speak. I force myself to write this letter to you. It is written badly. I see that I haven't found the correct register, that I haven't found the means to express what I am feeling. But I need to find some words, however paltry or inexact.

Of course, I don't need to tell you about the value of words, even in their most imprecise form, because you yourself are just beginning the long process of claiming language. First vowels, then consonants, your capacity for speech changes by the day. For you, language is still something precious, acquired with great effort. You know that it's a means to being understood, and you know—something that the rest of us have forgotten, but are now abruptly remembering— that it is a miracle to make yourself understood at all.

You are the most trusting person I know, but you are not at all certain of being understood. You are not always certain that the language you have at your disposal—of murmurs, of cries and babbles—is enough. You cry and you shout, and when that fails, you merely implore with your gaze. But you persevere, because instinct tells you that language is, for all its imperfections, integral to your survival. Language is how you will make the world around you. It is how you will make yourself.

You have faith in language, the precise faith that I now lack. Perhaps because of this, when I'm with you, time slows down. Lately, my heart is constantly racing. But when I'm with you, it slackens, and I feel so strongly that this slower tempo is worth fighting for. The other side moves with such rapidity and blind conviction that it's all too easy to feel we must do the same. *There is no time for complacency. There is no time for inaction.* This is undoubtedly true. But at the same time, we need to defend another way of thinking and being, one that allows for hesitation, for nuance and mutability.

I have a distrust of certitude, even when I agree with the essential position being advocated. I don't think the urgency of our situation means that we cannot afford uncertainty. I need to believe in the value of the doubt I now feel, in its ability to create a space for the slowness of thought and conviction. I need to believe in it, not least because it promotes thinking before acting—and if there is one thing we know about the president-elect, it is that he acts before he thinks.

I worry that you will grow up in a time of ideological haste, a time of wild conviction and coarsened thought. The truth is that they have already taken so much, and they will take much more. But I promise that I will do everything in my power to keep them from impoverishing the language you are fighting so hard for right now, from reducing your world to absolutes. Language has a generative power that is unparalleled in the world. I would like for you to grow up believing in this power, and the freedom it can afford. I would like for you to grow up with the faith you have right now.

YOU ARE MY KIND

iO Tillett Wright

I can see you, there, a sliver of your leg on the carpet visible through the bathroom door. You, with your sinewy frame and keen mind, waiting for your father to appear and give you something your mother can't. You, who will have grown up acclimated to an unorthodox way of naming things—addressing them as they live, rather than as they are classified by science, you think in a different way from most.

I don't know what you want, but I know I will probably cause in you the same urgent desire for approval my father created in me. You probably are waiting for my opinion, my direction, my collaboration on something. Maybe you want to tell me about a crush. Maybe you want to watch a show, play a video game, build something. Maybe you just want to spend time, and I will make a point of it.

Your world will be a free one. The circle of normalcy you will grow up in will include every kind of person, and so many animals. I will close the loop of neglect that can continue on like an unwieldy double helix if it isn't wrestled into submission. I will set meals in front of you, every day, growing your bones. I will tell you about every book I've read, every talk I've seen, and show you every landscape I've walked through. I will take you on trains through Europe, by camel to the Pyramids, and to swim within the glowing plankton in Puerto Rico's coastal bathtub. We will play soccer in the squares of Havana, and you will meet the street boys who taught me compassion. You will eat sea urchin in Italy and freeze your nuts off in Colorado.

You, as a tiny child, will see the ink on my forearm that tells you, over and over, that no matter what you are, no matter what you become, you are my kind. You will have a home, a meal, and a companion with me, at all times, anywhere.

You, your skin covered in nicks and marks from your explorations and adventures, will sit and wait for me, the dog in your lap, a finger scratching his chin. I will see you before you know I can, and I will admire your natural calm, your grace, your effortless presence. I think of the hatred in the world you will be born into, the shrinking resources, the overcrowding, the violence and division, and I get a pang of protectiveness in my heart. I will always take the job of protecting you very seriously.

As I swing the door open and greet you, you look up at me with eyes too knowing. You are witty. Your crack comes swiftly, and it lands.

Your sister is in the next room.

I will love these times, just you and me.

It's normal, you tell me, to have a spermless, dickless father. To have a father with scars where breasts once were and a forever sense of displacement, to be the grandchild of mental illness, and the heir to addiction's ravaging. It's no more extreme for you than my realities were for me. You will be well versed in my tale. You will have spent your life in handmade costumes, drinking tea that keeps you up for three days, going to the second half of Broadway shows, and being finger-fed broccoli doused in soy sauce and garlic by your grandmother. You will have seen her insane house. You will have put your tiny hand in mine countless times, intuitively aware that your parent needed a stabilizing reminder of his independence. You will have reminded me, since you were tiny, that I can scoop you up and we can leave if we need to. We are safe, because I made it safe. That hovel is not our home. We have our own warm, safe place to go back to. No one will shake either of us from our sleep with violence, because I won't allow it. You will remind me that I protect you, and always have.

You, raised by a tribe, aware of the beauty of multiplicity and difference, will bring something to those around you that others don't. You will know this and feel a sense of purpose because of it. You will be a testament to the fact that we can move toward each other and not fortify ourselves in echo chambers of like-minded politics. You will be eager to discuss, to listen, to learn.

I will look at you, sitting there, and, in your eyes, see a burning strength, a hunger for exploration, and I will feel grateful; grateful that we made you, so you can carry the tradition on, of radical acceptance. I will look into your calm face and at the dog completely surrendered to your affections, and I will understand that we will be fine. You are in charge now, thank god.

ZENAIDA

Francisco Goldman

My friend Axel was brought to the United States as a baby by parents fleeing the infernal war in Guatemala. He grew up in Jamaica, Queens, New York, and, at the age of thirty-five, was living in Long Island, working as an IT technician. He'd had two small children with his female partner. After he'd dropped his kids off at school on a morning when the roads were icy, he rear-ended a car driven by a white woman, and she phoned the police. Axel, still an undocumented immigrant, didn't have a driver's license. The police took him to the police station, where an ICE agent happened to be present. Two days later, Axel was deported to Guatemala, a country where he knew nobody and where even any documentation of his existence, such as a birth certificate, could no longer be found. But a *mara* street gang swiftly identified him as a lost deportee from the United States who spoke broken Spanish with a New York City accent and who didn't even understand where he was; the gang began to threaten and extort him, and Axel decided to get the hell out of there and flee north, just as his parents had done more than thirty years before. Axel has since endured an amazing but terrifying odyssey that I won't even try to describe here (I was introduced to Axel by the young anthropologist Levi Vonk, who has been chronicling Axel's story, often sharing adventures and mishaps at his side) apart from this one incident.

Having made the journey up through Mexico from Guatemala, Axel finally reached the border, where, as is customary, he paid off Zeta cartel emissaries to be allowed to cross into the USA. On the other side—that is, in U.S. territory—he was again blocked by Zetas, who demanded the safe passage password he'd been given on the other side. Axel gave it but was told it wasn't the right password. A Zeta with a nail bat attacked Axel, delivering blows that shattered his wrist and tore the skin and hair from the top of his head. There in the Texas desert, Axel was left for dead. But he somehow managed to get up and stagger forward for something like another twelve hours until he finally collapsed into unconsciousness. Sometime later, he was awoken by the kicks of a U.S. Border Patrol agent. After receiving some medical treatment, he was again swiftly deported for the second time in a year from the country that he'd lived in nearly all his life.

This Christmas Eve of 2016, Axel came to our apartment for dinner in Mexico City. He's been living here over the last months, barely scraping by, doing odd jobs such as washing dishes, blocked from being able to take on some of the computer tech support jobs he's been offered because he doesn't have papers. Long after midnight, as we sat up sipping mezcal, he began to talk about that first journey he'd taken through Mexico from Central America, on foot, sometimes on local buses, and by jumping aboard the freight train known as La Bestia, that so many hundreds of thousands of migrants have ridden on in recent years, a trek routinely marked for nearly everyone who undertakes it by violence, rapes, kidnappings, extortions, and other tragedies. Axel had seen a traveling companion lose his grip while trying to jump onto La Bestia and fall, sucked by the train's velocity beneath the freight car and into the path of its iron wheels, which sliced off his legs and, as the train roared away, probably ended his life. The worst thing he witnessed, though, said Axel, the incident that most haunted him, was when, in southern Mexico, he and another traveling companion were forced to take a long detour into the jungle in order to avoid an immigration police checkpoint they'd been told awaited ahead on the highway. If you've read Óscar Martínez's landmark chronicle *The Beast*[*] or have heard other veterans of the migrants' trail tell their stories, then you know that many of the journey's worst terrors lurk along the jungle paths and secluded ranchos of those unavoidable detours: vicious rural gangs, some associated with organized crime groups such as the Zetas, others with police. Through the vegetation, they glimpsed a group of men, including a young man who was obviously a fellow Central American migrant because he was the one being held with his arms wrenched behind his back, and heard

[*]   Its original title in Spanish is much better: *Los migrantes que no importan.*

the unspeakable sobbing and shrieks of female suffering, which told Axel and his friend what was happening there, what that Central American man was being forced to watch being done to the woman he'd been traveling with, perhaps his wife or a sister. Axel and his friend were only two, that Mexican gang numbered at least half a dozen, what could they do but continue on, he said, praying they wouldn't be noticed? That was the scene that still, of all the horrors he'd witnessed and experienced on the migrants' trail, most tormented Axel's memory and conscience.

Like I said, it was Christmas Eve. We didn't go to mass that night. I do not practice or identify with any one religion, but Axel's story did make me remember the priest's sermon that I'd listened to exactly one year before when I'd gone with my wife, Jovi, and her father and brother, both named Juan Carlos, to Midnight Mass at the Jesuit church a block and a half away from where we live in Colonia Roma. The priest talked about the meaning of the newborn Christ as being manifested in just that, his infant state, a fragile being who, even if he was the Son of God, was still utterly dependent on the care of others, which we should consider as also meaning, said the priest, dependent on the care of all of us. The priest turned this "infant Christ" into a metaphor for our shared human duty to always look out for and protect the defenseless, weak, and vulnerable, babies and children, of course, but not just them, anyone in danger of being overpowered by malevolent forces it would be impossible for him or her alone to resist.

Who is this letter for, then? To an imagined child—Zenaida I'll call you, because that's the name of one of

Jovi's closest friends, an undocumented Tlapaneca woman, an immigration activist herself now, living in New York. That horrific rape in the jungle occurred, and that's how you were engendered, Zenaida. Human rights organizations have estimated that as many as 80 percent of the Central American women who make the trip up through Mexico to the U.S. border suffer rapes and other kinds of sexual assault, commonly in circumstances similar to what Axel had witnessed. Many prepare beforehand by taking contraceptives, including injections and implants, meant to last for at least the length of the journey, but not all do. The savageries that humans inflict on weaker humans, there's nothing new about that, but nobody endures more of that at the hands of men than poor women from poor countries do. Checking into an abortion clinic just isn't a realistic option for most of the women who travel the migrants' trail, even if they do manage to reach the United States. Yes, I'm imagining that your mother miraculously survived, Zenaida, and that as broken as she was, she went on with her journey. But I won't dare to imagine or describe, certainly not here, what I mean by "broken." I guess it's just because I heard this story on Christmas Eve and associated it with that Jesuit priest's explication of that metaphor of the Infant Jesus that I couldn't help but imagine that it was your destiny to become a living infant yourself, Zenaida. Maybe your mother felt your own fragile newborn life to be an extension of her own precarious existence and of her near escape from death, and decided to love you fiercely. This story of your birth, Zenaida, isn't such an uncommon one; I've heard many stories. I have a friend who adopted a child born of just such a crime. Recalling the Jesuit priest's Christmas Eve sermon, it was impossible not to conjure you. Who could be more vulnerable, more in need of love and compassion, than you?

So this letter is to you, Zenaida, who may not exist, though many versions of you do, but it's also addressed to some other children and adolescents who I know do exist. I'm thinking of the children who attend the after-school learning sanctuary for immigrant children in Bushwick, Brooklyn, called Still Waters in a Storm, especially the core group of girls it's been my privilege and pleasure to mentor in creative writing one night a week for the past several years, beginning back when they were seven and eight, and who are now ten and eleven. It was early November when I received a fund-raising e-mail sent out by Still Waters that featured a photograph of Jannethy, one of those core girls, holding up a sign that read, I FEEL UPSET, SAD, WHEN DONALD TRUMP IS SO CLOSE TO WINNING THE ELECTION, IF HE DOES HE WILL DEPORT ALL MEXICANS BECAUSE MY RACE MATTERS. I'm thinking, too, of some of the adolescent, mostly Mayan and Guatemalan newly arrived immigrants I met a few months ago in New Bedford, Massachusetts, our country's largest fishing port—it's also where *Moby-Dick* begins—during a meeting in the offices of a union that protects the rights of Central American and other immigrant workers, documented or not, founded by Guatemalan labor activists there. The meeting was being held so that a human rights worker who'd come from Guatemala could share information on how DNA testing can help Guatemalans now living in the United States identify relatives lost during the three-decades-long Guatemalan internal war among the skeletal remains of the war's victims being continually unearthed by forensics teams from clandestine graves in that country. Guatemala's war formally ended in 1996, with a peace treaty between the victorious army and the crushed guerrilla forces. Not long after, the final report of a United Nations commission estimated that more than two hundred thousand civilians were murdered in that war and that 97 percent of the killings were carried out by U.S.-supported Guatemalan military forces, a state crime against humanity that the UN ruled to have been a genocide. Many of the Guatemalans at the meeting in New Bedford that day—teenagers and children, most accompanied by a parent—hadn't been born when that war ended. If they had relatives long lost to the war's massacres and repression—as most surely did—that wasn't what they wanted to talk about. As Jovi and I discovered as soon as the meeting was over and some of the young people approached us, they wanted to talk about their own experiences. Most had undertaken the same nightmare journey up through Mexico that Axel had made, and their stories, which they quietly shared with us, were every bit as nightmarish and staggering as the ones Axel had told.

All of the young immigrants I've mentioned, you who may exist and those who definitely do, are now destined to endure the dangers of the Trump presidency, for however long we're fated to have to endure it. Without a doubt, some of our families and individual lives are going to be shattered, as Axel's was. Of course, a lot of harm has already been done. Whenever I imagine myself the father of a small child whose emotional well-being or vulnerable self-esteem has been disturbed or harmed by Trump's racist diatribes or threats of mass deportations and Nazi-like labeling and registries, or by his repulsive denigration of women, or by the widespread racial bullying spawned by the public normalization of hate speech that the Trump phenomenon has brought about, I feel a deep and frightening violence within myself. This is inevitable, though it does need to be acknowledged, and of course, it has to be acknowledged, too, that such violent emotions aren't very fruitful or admirable, even if they aren't always completely useless either—such violent emotions can give you a jolt or scare you and push you to seek worthier solutions to your anger and fear, right?

Not since Hitler has any major Western country been governed by such an overt bigot as Trump, and probably not since Hitler by such an obviously emotionally and psychologically unbalanced person. (Whether you consider Italy a major power or not, Berlusconi, Trump's equal in greed and personal depravity, was a neofascist clown show in comparison to our new president, much less dangerous and more comical a figure than the dourly humorless Trump.) But we have to remember that Hitler came to power in very different historical circumstances, and with massive and sustained popular support. Trump's case isn't like that. He was lucky to win. We all know the many reasons for that. (Russians; Comey; young people of all colors, including whites, voted uniformly against Trump, but just too many us, of all ages and from all ethnicities, decided not to come out to vote that day; many feel the Democrats nominated the wrong candidate; and so on.) By the time you are old enough to vote, Zenaida, Trump will be an ugly and distant memory, though I hope you'll know what a turning point he represented. His victory was the defiant expression of a clear minority of American voters, a last stand, or desperate tantrum, on behalf of a white supremacist United States and all its sclerotic old nationalist and imperial myths that have long been at the heart of our country's politics and the exercising of its power. But if we look into the future, Zenaida, we know what happened next. From the moment Trump was elected, so many of the rest of us were roused to begin looking for ways to overcome our fear and revulsion, and to think about and imagine and finally work toward achieving the kind of country we want to live in, one that more accurately represents us than this one brought about in 2016 does, one that doesn't exclude anybody apart from those who want to institutionalize exclusion and hate.

It has been kind of entertaining to watch the pundits in the elite media flailing to convince "us," but really themselves, that racism wasn't a decisive factor in Trump's victory. SORRY, LIBERALS. BIGOTRY DIDN'T ELECT DONALD TRUMP was the headline of an op-ed in *The New York Times* that I read the other day. But in that same edition, I read a report that identified immigration as the single issue that provided Trump with his edge in the electoral college—oh, right, I see, and bigotry has nothing to do with that particular issue, right? Of course, many of us are immune to the hermetic blather of the political pundits who infest our media; we know in our guts and, of course, in our families and communities what really happened. Sorry, pundit-cito, but if you acquiescently support a candidate who openly indulges in racist hate speech, you're complicit in that racism no matter what else you want to say about it. Anyway, didn't we all grow up in a country where parents, teachers, religious leaders (supposedly) taught us that racism was wrong, and didn't any of that mean a damned thing? Interestingly, on that same day the *Times* published a front-page investigative report that undercut another Trumpian myth—the one that blames a lawless U.S. border solely on rampant "bad hombres" from "Mexico" who could easily be kept out by his Wall—by exposing the corruption of U.S. border authorities by drug cartels and immigrant traffickers. As the prominent Mexican immigration activist Father Alejandro Solalinde has been saying all along, no Wall, however Big and Hideous, is ever going to be able to control who or what comes and goes across the U.S.-Mexico border. That power, Solalinde has said, rests solely in the hands of the organized crime cartels whose infinite power to corrupt on both sides of the border draws its strength from the insatiable appetite for drugs on the U.S. side and for the U.S. appetite for arms deals and profits, too. What were those Zetas who nearly murdered Axel doing on the Texas side of the U.S. border? How did they get there? Who really gives the orders around there?

The other day, reading *The Story of the Lost Child*, the final volume of Elena Ferrante's magnificent Neapolitan Quartet, I came across this reflection by the narrator: "In the wealthier countries a mediocrity that hides the horrors of the rest of the world has prevailed." Understanding that mediocrity, Zenaida, is a key to grasping the truth of Trump, and to protecting yourself, and rising above, far above, the lies, slanders, and threats directed against you and your families throughout the horrible months of the 2016 electoral campaign. In some ways, mediocrity is even more despicable than evil. Evil has a plan: it can be adroitly wielded like the deadliest poisoned knife blade; it can purchase a television network, politicians, even an election; it knows how to make billions and billions of dollars every day and divide it up among just a few; it can even rape and sexually assault and boast and lie about it later, confident of the protection afforded by its wealth, privilege, and impunity. But mediocrity is lazy, cowardly, and easily manipulated and is much more common than evil—it's fucking everywhere. We'd be in danger of drowning in it if we somehow forgot—but we sure won't—to get up off our knees.

To rise above your enemies—by which I mean Trump and anyone else who would harm or diminish you in the name of the essentially white nationalist and ultimately doomed political movement he represents—Zenaida, and you, too, Zenaida's somewhat older sisters and brothers whom I'm also addressing, you need to understand who you are, where you came from, and also where your parents came from, why they often left your countries behind before you did, and how those countries got that way. You need to know your history, that's all I mean. You probably already do, and understand all of this better than I do; but just in case you don't or have allowed that knowledge to slip from your mind because you've been distracted by other pressing matters, the few stories I've shared in this letter so far, about Axel, about your mother and father, about Jannethy and those kids in New Bedford, offer plenty of clues and pieces of evidence for what I want to say, and you probably don't need me to connect the dots. Your parents, and then you, too, fled countries ravaged by U.S.-sponsored, historically unjustifiable geopolitical "proxy wars" that not only targeted rebels and peaceful political dissenters in your countries but also largely defenseless civilian populations. In Guatemala, El Salvador, and Honduras especially—Nicaragua is a different kind of calamity—fragile social fabrics and democratic political institutions, where these existed at all, were corrupted and destroyed, replaced by even more extreme cultures of poverty, violence, crime, and corruption, whether ruled over by depraved *mara* street gangs or organized crime governments and the ever-more empowered greedy economic elites who were there all along. Mexico, or much of Mexico, is now in some ways in even worse shape. We may feel kindly toward President Obama—there is so much to admire about him as a man, I agree, though it's not like he didn't earn his title of Deporter in Chief, and so on— but a principal reason that Axel and so many others before and since have had to make that long, perilous detour into the jungle to evade a highway checkpoint manned by often criminal police was Obama's so-called Plan Sur, which has literally outsourced immigration enforcement to corrupt Mexican authorities, providing Mexico with millions and millions of dollars to hunt and deport—effectively to hunt, rape, rob, extort, murder, and maybe deport—Central American migrants in its southern regions in an attempt to alleviate the embarrassment of having hundreds of thousands of child refugees massing at our borders, fleeing the violence and poverty of the very same Central American countries we gifted with "democracy" in exchange for helping to turn their countries into mass graves back in the '80s. (It's not just me who says so. Far from it. For example, read Nicholas Kristof's op-eds on Plan Sur and the Central American migrant crisis in *The New York Times*.)

It so happens that I'm the son of a Central American immigrant, Yolanda Molina Hernandez, who never had to make any long journey on foot, granted, but who quietly put up with her share of shit in her many years of living in the Commonwealth of Massachusetts and who never let her son forget for a second that "eres guatemalteco también, hijo," and that son sure never did. You can even say that "not forgetting" has largely propelled the narrative of his adult life. This summer when I went back to Guatemala, as I do at least once a year, I visited some of the towns in the department of Quiché that many immigrants to New Bedford come from. Zacualpa is one of those towns. Starting in 1981, when the population of Zacualpa was eighteen thousand, the town endured so many Guatemalan army massacres that by 1983, only two families were still living there. The rest had either been killed or fled. The army used the convent of the local parish church as a torture center. That was why, as the human rights investigator and photographer Jean-Marie Simon first reported, after people began returning to the town, they refused to attend mass in that church, as if they regarded it as having been possessed by the devil. Back in 1984, Jean-Marie took this testimony from a man who until recently had been a resident of the town: "At first they killed people inside the convent, where no one could see. Eventually, however, they began to line them up in front of the ceiba tree in the main square, and simply shot people in plain view of anyone who happened to be there. Once, the army started shooting from the air: there were so many bullets flying that my aunt said it looked like beans raining down."

Jean-Marie was traveling with Jovi and me when we went to Zacualpa last summer. We found a town that now commemorates the tragedies of thirty years ago and its dead while also embracing the challenges of the present. That same church is a busy community hub again; in that convent, there's a haunting shrine to the victims tortured and killed and even in some cases buried there. In the same parish building, nuns have opened an office that serves as a center for the families of immigrants to the United States. From there, through a network of organizations and offices extending up through Mexico and the United States, people can try to locate missing relatives. Maps are given out depicting where migrant shelters and other aid can be found on the migrants' trail through Mexico, along with brochures and documents providing other useful information and warnings. Wives and female relatives left behind by husbands and sons who've gone ahead to the United States hold meetings there, and have formed a weaving and crafts collective. All over town, though, there were also signs of the relative economic bustle driven by the money sent back by town residents who've found work in the United States: all those new second and even third stories built over often picturesque older houses like cinderblock Lego constructions. The town is still poor, but, thanks to the steady flow of *remisa* payments, it's much better off than it was in the war years. As Jean-Marie pointed out there and in other similar towns, you don't see children with hair falling out from malnutrition all over the place anymore. You do see a startling number of new pickup trucks with Statue of Liberty and U.S. flag decals on their bumpers and windshields. Far away in New Bedford, many of the immigrants from Zacualpa work in that historic port city's fish processing plants, the kind of cold, wet, smelly, bloody, hard, dreary job that epitomizes the class of work established American workers are said to now spurn. A fish processing plant I visited there was displaying in its lobby the championship trophy of a local soccer league won by the team sponsored by that plant: the team's name, printed on the trophy's plaque, was the Zacualpa Futbol Club. New Bedford is where, in March 2007, the notorious ICE immigration raid, one of the largest ever in the United States, took place at the Michael Bianco textile plant, where the immigrant workers were producing armored vests for U.S. soldiers fighting in Afghanistan and Iraq. Three hundred sixty-one immigrants were detained, many from Guatemala; mothers were suddenly separated from their children that day and sent to detention centers as far away as Texas; many were deported. The New Bedford immigrant community was badly wounded by that raid, and the climate of daily insecurity and fear hanging over many families darkened, but it was also when the community began to organize itself as never before. Every year, the anniversary of the raid is commemorated in New Bedford churches and homes and elsewhere there, a communal reminder of the risks and hardships endured by Guatemalan and other undocumented immigrants, and a reaffirmation of why they've chosen that hard path. It's obvious: to give their families, here in the States and back home, a chance for a better life, for better wages, for better educations and opportunities.

Not far from Zacualpa, in the middle of a highway traffic rotary outside the city of Quetzaltenango, there stands an enormous, heroic statue of a young man with a small backpack over his shoulder, striding northward, a statue put up recently, honoring the bravery and sacrifice of the country's migrants. It doesn't really matter what Trump does; young men and women and even children will keep setting off for the United States, even though most know about the dangers and struggles that lie ahead on the journey through Mexico and on both sides of the Mexico-U.S. borderlands. Because nothing is ever so simple as that, there are also migrants who feel pressured to do "the right thing" and head north even if they don't want to, or who actually don't understand what they're getting into, many led astray by unscrupulous loan sharks and coyotes. But that singular statue was put up because it represents a truth that that community agrees on: the migrant's journey is heroic, and it is heroic because it is carried out on behalf of others, for families and communities. That was your mother's journey, Zenaida, however it may have ended. I have a weird faith that you made it and that you will grow up feeling treasured, knowing that you incarnate and represent the meaning of that journey, somehow feeling strengthened, not crushed, by that terrible knowledge as well.

The founding director of the miraculous Still Waters, Stephen Haff, has recently conceived of a new project for some of the students who attend that after-school learning sanctuary. They are translating *Don Quixote* into English, while inserting stories from their own families' lives into their translations. It seems a perfect way to understand those lives, merging them to that epic of inspired folly, daring, struggle, ardor, madness, poetry, love, courage, and fantastic transformations, in a sense newly universalizing that classic and endlessly expansive narrative by truly—that is, also somewhat subversively—Americanizing it. Zenaida, Jannethy, you beautiful and damaged teenage heroes I met in New Bedford, and Axel, too, whether or not you ever make it back to the States and to your own children, your stories will never cease to be told. In transforming your lives, you and your families are slowly transforming this difficult United States of ours, too. Nobody is more deserving of being listened to, of being cherished and admired, than you.

STAY OPEN

Celeste Ng

My darling boy,

You are such a kind child. You've been kind since birth. You used to cry when other babies at day care cried, even if you were snuggled in your favorite teacher's lap. You used to ask me to skip the pages of the book where the problems happened: where Goldilocks breaks Baby Bear's chair, where Eeyore's tail falls off, where Max tells his mother he'll eat her up. It was too painful for you to see those things happen. Even now, at six, sometimes you still bury your face in my shoulder at those moments. It's one of my favorite things about you: your huge heart.

But that huge heart makes you vulnerable. When there's too much—too much fear, too much pain, too much *feeling*—you try to shrink away, to hide. You've always loved turtles, and I think I know why: you have the same tendency they do, to retreat inside yourself in the face of trouble. Except you, sweet boy, have no shell, and the rain and stones and thorns find you anyway; even rolled up tight, you are just as tender outside as you are in.

This has been fine, so far, because we live in an unusual place. It's the closest place I can find to the world I want you to live in, a kind and gentle place, an accepting place. I don't think you realize yet how unusual it is. So many things in your life—that our city observes Indigenous Peoples' Day instead of Columbus Day, that your school gets vacation for Easter *and* Rosh Hashanah *and* Eid, that five families on our two-block street are mixed race—are so different from most of our country. To you they seem as completely natural and unremarkable as your friend Harper, who has a Mommy and a Mama, or your friend Christopher, who likes to wear dresses, or your kindergarten classmates with names from Hannah to Tigerlily to Amadou, or their parents who come to pickup wearing hijabs or suits or hoodies or, in one case, sleeve tattoos.

Your father and I chose to raise you here because we wanted you to meet lots of people who aren't like you, and you do. So sometimes you ask big questions, and I try to put big answers into words small enough for you to understand. We were running errands, and you said suddenly, *What's gay?* You'd heard it on the car radio: marriage equality had just passed, and some people were upset. I told you it was when men loved men or women loved women, and that some people didn't like that, and you said, with a defiant thrust of your little jaw, *Well, I think it's fine.* You saw my sweatshirt that read FEMINIST and asked what it meant, and I said, Someone who thinks women are just as good as men, and you thought for a minute and said, genuinely puzzled, *Why would people think they weren't?* Another day, you asked what *black* and *white* meant, and I told you, and then I told you that some people thought people with darker skin like you and me weren't as good as people with lighter skin like Daddy, and you said, voice dripping with scorn, *Well, that's not right,* and I said, I know, I *know,* and I was so proud of your big heart, how ridiculous this all seemed to you.

But even we don't live in a bubble. I knew this, of course, but in the past few weeks, I've had to face it more and more. A week or so after the election, an elderly woman in our neighborhood was pushed to the ground by two strangers shouting, *You didn't vote for Trump!* The house next door had a Clinton sign in the window, the woman had been taking her garbage to the curb, the men had assumed the sign was hers. The news all across the country was full of these stories. Soon you're going to realize how hard so much of the world is, even our town, and these days, I sometimes wish I could give you a shell, or at least a thick, leathery hide, anything that would protect you more than your soft child skin.

In less fearful moments, though, this is what I want to tell you: Resist the urge to grow a shell. Don't let fear convince you that hardness is good.

We've heard so much lately about barring certain people, deporting other people, building an actual wall to keep still others out. We've heard people—who are now running our government—mock those in need, those with disabilities, those who dare to admit they struggle or hurt or have been hurt. It would be easier in some ways, wouldn't it, to not care so much, for pain and fear and sadness to bounce off us like bullets off Superman's chest. But the thing about shells — and walls—is that they keep out so many good things, too. Staying open makes you vulnerable, yes, but it also makes space for kindness and gentleness and compassion.

The other day, I told you our family motto was *Be kind, be curious, be helpful.* Kindness and helpfulness you understood right away. Then you asked, *Why is curious in there?*

Because being curious is admitting that you don't know, but also that you want to know. That what you don't know is worth knowing. That people you don't know are worth knowing, that they have something to teach you. That learning about them—that encountering new ideas—doesn't threaten you, it enriches you. That what you haven't experienced is worth experiencing. That you approach the world as a trove of things to take in, rather than things you frantically, fearfully wall out. *Be kind, be curious, be helpful*: what that really means is, *stay open.*

This will be so important for the next few years, but really it goes beyond this election, the new administration, whatever may come after that. It's about the kind of person I hope you'll grow up to be, the kind of country I hope you get to live in, the kind of world I hope you'll help make.

So let me tell you one more thing. It's something I remind myself, when confronted with hate and fear, something that I hope you keep in mind in this new era and always. Every one of those conversations you and I have had—about being gay, being feminist, being black or being white—ended with the same question. *But why would people think that?* you asked every time, and every time, I gave you the same answer: *Because they're afraid. Because it's different from what they grew up thinking, and it's a new idea, and sometimes new things are scary.* Like the first time you went swimming, I tell you, or that time you tried rock climbing, or the first time we went in a plane. You'd never done it before, and you thought it would be scary. *But then I realized it wasn't,* you say, and I say, Exactly.

RAMBLING THOUGHTS FOR ROSCOE

Peter Orner

My son, Roscoe, was born on October 22, 2016. He's named after Roscoe Conway, the title character of William Kennedy's 2002 novel, *Roscoe*. It's my brother's favorite book. My brother names all my kids. Phoebe's named after Holden's favorite (only?) sister. We've always been a family with an undue faith in literature. Roscoe Conway is a decent, extremely lovable—if fundamentally corrupt—politician in Albany, New York, in the 1920s. The birth of Roscoe Conway's namesake wasn't easy. Our Roscoe's heart rate went way down shortly before his delivery. A very anxious half hour later, he arrived. Except he was silent. Utterly. He's my second kid. I knew the drill, at least I thought I did. He slid into the hands of the waiting midwife, purple, bloody, squished together. And I breathed and awaited the beat. You know? I awaited the beat for him to . . . and there was nothing. Zero. No scream. No cry. No whimper. Instead of handing the baby to Katie, the midwife handed him to the doctor—called in because of his drop in heart rate—who immediately brought him over to a table in the corner of the delivery room and proceeded to give him oxygen with a small handheld respirator. He also began to flick his feet with his index finger. The nurse who was next to the doctor did the same thing. She flicked his feet with her finger. You know how I mean? Like you might in high school when you want to wake up the friend who dozed off in the seat in front of you. And maybe that doesn't wake him up, so you set your index finger against your thumb and really fucking flick this time. That's how they flicked my kid's feet. They flicked those little purple feet, feet that had never walked anywhere, feet that didn't even know they were feet, with purpose. They flicked in near anger. I stood there dumbfounded, mute. This? This is modern medicine in 2016? You flick the feet? I looked over at Katie on the other side of the room. The nurses were attending to her. She was, of course, exhausted, relieved, broken, happy, dazed. I waved to get her attention and mouthed, *Something's wrong. I mean seriously something's really wrong. They're flicking his feet like he's—*

And you know what she said? Exhausted, dazed, broken, she said from across the room, in the calmest possible voice, "Talk to him. He knows your voice. Talk to him."

I swear, and I'm not proud of this, I mouthed back, *About what?*

There was this little guy on the table getting his feet flicked and he still wasn't reacting and he still wasn't screaming and he was my son, my own son, seconds, minutes old, and I had no idea what on earth to say to him. Is this even believable? I don't believe it myself. But here's as close as

I can come to the truth about what had to have been the worst moment of my life so far. He was my son, and I was already ashamed of him for not acting like the right kind of kid. For not screaming, for hardly breathing. For needing help breathing.

"Roscooooooe," Katie cooed from across the room. "Roscooooooe."

And the kid, he shifted his head a little toward the voice. It was the first sentient thing he did. The first alive thing. He did know her voice. I'm not a very sentimental person. This might be pretty obvious now. But I'll just say it. It was the most beautiful thing I've ever seen. He acknowledged his mother's voice. Ended up spending the next three days in the NICU. Little tubes in both nostrils. He looked like a little scuba diver. Now he screams all the time. Never bothers me at all. That's a lie. But I do hear those screams a little differently because they are evidence of how far he's already come and—who knows?—of how far he'll go.

There's a lot of despairing lately. A lot of shouting from the rooftops, too. Lot of hysteria on social media. Lot of gloom and doom in conversation. God knows I indulge myself in both. No hyperbole seems to go far enough. I want to say: *this, too, shall pass* even though I know it won't. That this truly is different, truly unprecedented. All the obvious things. I'm so tired of saying obvious things, and yet here I am, saying obvious things. I want to say that it must act as some kind of wake-up call, even though I already wonder about the sense of complacency that is already setting in. Just the other day, a writer friend of mine, who swore up and down, backward and forward, that he's not a racist, told me, hey, just give the president-elect a chance. At least he's going to shake things up, my friend said. This is what we are up against. Not the overt racists. It's the ones who claim they aren't. Who genuinely believe that using racism to get elected is only a means to an end. I encouraged my friend to reread, since I gave him the benefit of the doubt that maybe he'd read it, King's "Letter from Birmingham Jail." He said, I love that story!

And maybe it comes down to this. That King's impassioned plea to so-called white moderates to summon some moral gumption in the name of Jesus, in the name of humanity—is only a story.

Only a story?

Hell, call it a story. Stories are what I live by. And stories—like King's—are what I cling to now more than ever. And you might think this is cheesy, but the other night, in honor of the story!—"Letter from Birmingham Jail"—I read the letter, as I'd seen Anna Deavere Smith read it onstage a couple of years ago, to my drowsy six-year-old daughter, who, at first, protested—she wanted to hear *The Princess in Black and the Hungry Bunny Horde* again—but eventually I lulled her with the cadence of King's words and, finally, she fell asleep.

I have traveled the length and breadth of Alabama, Mississippi and all the other southern states. On sweltering summer days and crisp autumn mornings I have looked at the South's beautiful churches with their lofty spires pointing heavenward. I have beheld the impressive outlines of her massive religious education buildings. Over

and over I have found myself asking: "What kind of people worship here? Who is their God? Where were their
voices when the lips of Governor Barnett dripped with
words of interposition and nullification? Where were
they when Governor Wallace gave a clarion call for defi-
ance and hatred?"

I'm starting her on King's love early. Will it do any good
in the long run? Will she ever look up at the lofty spires of
churches and wonder if the beauty on the outside corre-
sponds to what sort of people worship inside?

God, I hope so.

I'm writing these thoughts in a coffee shop in Black
Mountain, North Carolina. I just heard one guy ask another
guy how the painting's going. The other guy answered with
a question:

"You know what the problem with painting is?"

"What?"

"It makes everything else look like crap."

Lot of wisdom in that. I'm not exactly sure how it applies
to our current situation, but something tells me it does.
That rectifying the damage that has been done is going to
take more than painting it over? That we've got to rebuild
the house in another spirit?

We'll see.

I'm going to put my faith in stories. All kinds of stories.

And the story of fall 2016 will always be, for me, a
minutes-old child recognizing his mother's voice as he
struggles for breath.

QUERIDÍSIMA PALOMITA: A LETTER TO MY GREAT-GREAT-GREAT-GREAT-GREAT-GRANDDAUGHTER

Cristina García

Muy querida nietecita,

I am writing to you from some two hundred years (or more) earlier than your birth. What I wouldn't give to have been there, or at the birth of each of the previous six, bighearted women who preceded you. Why six? Because I am trying to imagine a world, *your world*, seven generations from now. Why bighearted? Because I trust the long line of women originating with Pilar Akiko García-Brown (b. 1992), my own luminous daughter and your great-great-great-great-grandmother. I want to believe—believe fervently—that bigheartedness is a trait that can be passed on and lived fully, along with other precious bequeathals: generosity, spiritual beauty, creativity, a sense of humor, gentleness, a concern for others, hope, tolerance, a seeking nature, the ability to forgive, strength, vulnerability, encouragement, curiosity, sensuality, adventure, protectiveness, and a love for nature and all its creatures.

May I call you Palomita? Yes, Little Dove. Bringer of peace. In its plural form—*palomitas*—it means *popcorn* in Spanish. Do you speak Spanish? Other languages? Recently, I permitted myself an alter ego for the long-denied painter in me and named her Eva Perdíz, after a blue-headed quail dove in Cuba, where I was born. It is an endangered species, like so many others in our flailing world. What is your universe like, dearest child of the future? Is it, too, endangered? I am trying to bring it into focus, but it isn't easy. Civilizations can last long and die hard. Change is often more convulsive than gradual; war, sadly, easier than peace. Are such painful derailments necessary for growth? Sometimes I think about how the end of World War II was a mere seventy years ago. How the world, as everyone understood it then, was believed to be over. Today, the times feel disturbingly similar, apocalyptic. And yet, I remind myself, humanity went on after 1945 and continued forging ahead in the face of ever-greater atrocities, to keep rebuilding anew.

Is your planet warmer and wetter than mine? Have the decisions we fought against, fought *for*, yielded a more just and verdant world? Have you read about our desperate times in your history books? *Are* there books? I hope technology isn't holding you hostage the way it does so many of us today, fracturing our concentration, keeping us neglectful of those we love, surrendering our time to its empty seductions. Do you follow the cycles of the moon? The seasons? Are there breezes to cool your brow? I ask you because we are on the cusp, as I write today, of very bad times, querida nietecita, when the forces of destruction are lining up to dismantle and trample our very basic, hard-won rights. Why must we keep traveling full circle to ground zero? Reinventing ourselves to the same sacred places? I worry about what today's devastations will push forward to your generation, seven generations from now.

Can you take *any* rights for granted, darling Palomita? Is there still injustice in your world? Poverty? Inequality? Racism? How can we move ahead and trust that our progress is real, irreversible, that we don't have to keep fighting the same battles again and again? Or is that the nature of guarding one's rights, preventing us from ever taking them for granted (not even for a moment, it seems)? But there are things we should be able to take for granted, don't you think?

Is your air clean enough to breathe? Your water fresh enough to drink? Can you love whomever you want without fear or discrimination? Walk the streets freely? Do good work and get paid fairly for it? Is your body your own domain? Are you at liberty to decide the children you will bear, or not? Can loved ones and strangers alike travel openly across borders? How is the education in your time? Nowadays, young people like you are overly burdened with the financial debts from their studies. Can you imagine how unscrupulous it is to profit from another's desire for learning, for betterment? Seven generations from mine to yours. How much has everything changed?

Yes, there is heartlessness in my world, dulce Palomita, but there is also beauty. A few days ago, I took a long hike in the woods near my home. It had been raining hard, after many years of drought in California, and the streams rushed with water, neon yellow-orange mushrooms sprouted everywhere, and others—nestled along the fallen trunks of redwood trees—were dark and leathery looking, as if sun cured, yet as soft as I imagine your cheek to be. I spotted, too, a small, unexpected waterfall. It was hypnotic. Seven generations from my world to yours. Does any of this still exist for you?

The constitution of the Iroquois nation—sometimes known as the Great Law of the Iroquois—says, in part, that its people should "have always in view not only the past and present but also coming generations, even those whose faces are yet beneath the surface of the ground—the unborn of the future." And yet I see your face somehow, Palomita, round and gentle as my own daughter's. It isn't easy to change the world, corazón. No easier for you in your time than it is for us in ours. But what I wish for you is to keep trying, nietecita mía, perpetuating our most precious bequeathals, living with grace and dignity and passion—and ensuring these possibilities for all. Keep trying, too, for the seven generations who will come after you, and after them, and after them again. Sí, I wish for you adventure and loving protection both—and for you to help sustain the unbroken chain of hope.

Sending all my love to you in the future,
Tu abuelita Cristina

Postscript

SIGNS FROM THE WOMEN'S MARCH

Carolina De Robertis

JANUARY 21, 2017—OAKLAND, CALIFORNIA

My vagina has a lot to say
Fuck your patriarchy / We are the resistance
I don't usually make signs but WTF? / OMG GOP WTF?
Love not hate makes America great / OK ladies now
    get in formation
Together we rise / There's no Planet B / Big trouble
    in little hands
I'm a feminist what's your superpower? / I'll grab my own
Fight for democracy / Fight like a girl
Donald, duck!

We need a president who reads books and I can't believe
    I had to make this sign

Nyet

Amazon womyn rise / That's Reverend Nasty to you
I'm with her & her & her & her & her & her & her
    & her & her

Our rights are not up for grabs and neither are we
Don't fuck with my flower / This pussy bites back
This trans pussy bites back / Together we rise
Protests are for pussies / I am not your negro
Este pendejo no me representa / My headscarf

is not a weapon

Make America think again
You can't comb over climate change
BLOTUS Biggest Liar of the United States
If my uterus were a corporation would you regulate it?
Rage rage against the dying of the light / Stay fucking mad
Old hippies never die, they just get new knees and keep on
    marching
I know signs. I make the best signs. They're terrific.
    Everybody agrees. Trust me.

Viva la vulva
We can we will
This is the heartland
Make racists afraid again
For my daughter I won't go back

They tried to bury us they didn't know we were seeds
    (Mexican proverb)
I have been to the future and

we won

    Resist defend love
    The seas are rising but so are we

ACKNOWLEDGMENTS

I wish to thank, first and foremost, each and every contributor to this book. It has been an honor and a joy to bear witness to your brilliance, generosity, and faith in both humanity and the written word. You inspire me more than I can say. I'll be forever grateful to you for saying *yes*, not only to this project but also to love and to dissent and to the work before us.

I also wish to thank my agent, Victoria Sanders, for everything and, above all, for believing in this idea a few minutes into its existence when it was still wild and unformed. I thank Bernadette Baker-Baughman, Chris Kepner, and Jessica Spivey, in my agent's office, for their talent and tireless work, as well as Deirdre Smerillo for her finesse and kind support.

A deep bow to Carole Baron (my gifted and indefatigable editor for nine years), Sonny Mehta, Anne Messitte, Genevieve Nierman, Jennifer Marshall, Russell Perreault, Barbara Richard, Beth Lamb, Megan Wilson, Jaclyn Whalen, and Tom Pold, and the rest of the remarkable Knopf and Vintage teams who worked so hard, and so diligently, to bring this book into the world. Gratitude also goes to Virago in the United Kingdom and to the visionary Sarah Savitt, in particular, for opening doors to this book.

On a personal note, I thank my family for making it possible for me to sustain intensive focus on this project, especially my wife, Pamela Harris, and my mother-in-law-and-more-than-law, Margo Edwards. As to my children, Luciana and Rafael: this book is for everyone, but it is also for you—for your generation, for those to follow, and for the world you all deserve.

ABOUT THE CONTRIBUTORS

Elmaz Abinader's most recent poetry collection, *This House, My Bones*, was the Editor's Choice for 2014 from Willow Books / Aquarius Press. Her books include a memoir, *Children of the Roojme: A Family's Journey from Lebanon*, and a book of poetry, *In the Country of My Dreams . . .*, which won the PEN Oakland/Josephine Miles Award. Her plays include *Ramadan Moon*, *32 Mohammeds*, and *Country of Origin*. She is a frequent contributor to Al Jazeera English and has been anthologized widely. Elmaz is one of the cofounders of the Voices of Our Nations Arts Foundation (VONA/Voices), a writing workshop for writers of color. She teaches at Mills College. Find her at www.elmazabinader.com.

Faith Adiele has authored two memoirs, *The Nigerian-Nordic Girl's Guide to Lady Problems* and *Meeting Faith*, a spiritual memoir that won the PEN/Open Book Award. She is the writer/narrator/subject of *My Journey Home*, a PBS documentary about her international family, and has written for *The Rumpus*; *O, The Oprah Magazine*; *Transition*; and *Yes!* magazine. Chosen by *Marie Claire* magazine as "One of Five Women to Learn From," she has worked as a community activist, Buddhist nun, and college professor, teaching personal narrative at the Esalen Institute, VONA/Voices, and around the globe. Find her at www.adiele.com and @meetingfaith.

Jeff Chang is the author of *We Gon' Be Alright: Notes on Race and Resegregation, Who We Be: A Cultural History of Race in Post–Civil Rights America*, and *Can't Stop Won't Stop: A History of the Hip-Hop Generation*, which won the American Book Award and the Asian American Literary Award. He has been a USA Ford Fellow in Literature and was named by the *Utne Reader* one of "50 Visionaries Who Are Changing Your World." Chang has written extensively for *The Guardian*, *The Nation*, and *The New York Times*, among other publications. He is the executive director of the Institute for Diversity in the Arts at Stanford University.

Aya de León teaches creative writing at University of California–Berkeley. Kensington Books published her debut feminist heist novel, *Uptown Thief*, in 2016. The Justice Hustlers series will continue with *The Boss* in 2017 and *The Accidental Mistress* in 2018. Her work has also appeared in *Ebony*, *Guernica*, *Writer's Digest*, *Bitch*, and *The Huffington Post* and on *Def Poetry*. She blogs and tweets about culture, gender, and race at @AyadeLeon and www.ayadeleon.com. She is also at work on a social justice children's picture book series and a YA black girl spy novel.

Junot Díaz was born in the Dominican Republic and raised in New Jersey. He is the author of the critically acclaimed *Drown*; *The Brief Wondrous Life of Oscar Wao*, which won the 2008 Pulitzer Prize and the National Book Critics Circle Award; and *This Is How You Lose Her*, a *New York Times* bestseller and National Book Award finalist. He is the recipient of a MacArthur Fellowship, PEN/Malamud Award, Dayton Literary Peace Prize, Guggenheim Fellowship, and PEN/O. Henry Award. A graduate of Rutgers University, Díaz is currently the fiction editor at *Boston Review* and the Rudge and Nancy Allen Professor of Writing at MIT.

Mona Eltahawy is an award-winning Egyptian American feminist writer and commentator, and the author of *Headscarves and Hymens: Why the Middle East Needs a Sexual Revolution*. Her essays and op-eds on Egypt, the Islamic world, and women's rights have appeared in various publications, including *The Washington Post* and *The New York Times*. She has appeared as a guest commentator on MSNBC, BBC, CNN, PBS, Al Jazeera, NPR, and dozens of other television and radio networks, and she is a contributing opinion writer for *The International New York Times*. She lives in Cairo and New York City.

Boris Fishman is the author of *A Replacement Life* and *Don't Let My Baby Do Rodeo*, both *New York Times* Notable Books of the Year. He has won the Sophie Brody Medal from the American Library Association and the VCU Cabell First Novelist Award. His journalism, essays, and criticism have appeared in *The New Yorker*, *The New York Times Magazine* and *Book Review*, *The Guardian*, *Travel + Leisure*, and *New York* magazine, among other publications. His next book is a work of creative nonfiction about food and identity.

He lives in New York City and teaches creative writing at Princeton University.

Parnaz Foroutan is the author of *The Girl from the Garden* and has received fellowships and awards from PEN Center USA Emerging Voices, Hedgebrook, and the Elizabeth George Foundation, among other institutions. She currently lives in Los Angeles with her husband and two daughters.

Karen Joy Fowler is the author of six novels and three short story collections, including the *New York Times* bestseller and *New York Times* Notable Book *The Jane Austen Book Club*. Her most recent novel, *We Are All Completely Beside Ourselves*, won the 2014 PEN/Faulkner Award and the California Book Award and was shortlisted for the Man Booker Prize in 2014. She's written literary, contemporary, historical, and science fiction. She lives in Santa Cruz, California.

Cristina García is the award-winning author of seven novels, including *Dreaming in Cuban*, *The Agüero Sisters*, *Monkey Hunting*, *A Handbook to Luck*, *The Lady Matador's Hotel*, *King of Cuba*, and the forthcoming *Here in Berlin*. She has edited anthologies, written children's books, and published poetry. García's work has been nominated for a National Book Award and translated into fourteen languages. She lives in the San Francisco Bay Area.

Alicia Garza is an organizer, writer, freedom dreamer, and cofounder of #BlackLivesMatter, an international organizing network developed after the murder of Trayvon Martin, focused on combating anti-Black racism in all its forms. She has been the recipient of numerous awards and accolades for her organizing work, including being named on the Root 100 2015 list of African American achievers and influencers between the ages of twenty-five and forty-five, as one of the 2016 "Women of the Year" by *Glamour*, and among the "World's Greatest Leaders" in 2016 by *Fortune*. Her writing has been featured in publications such as *The Guardian*, *The Nation*, *The Feminist Wire*, and *Truthout*, among others.

Francisco Goldman is the author of *Say Her Name* (2011), winner of the Prix Femina Étranger, and three other novels and two nonfiction books, including *The Interior Circuit: A Mexico City Chronicle* (2014). These have been translated into fifteen languages. He has received a Cullman Center Fellowship, a Guggenheim Fellowship, and a Berlin Prize, among other awards. His work has appeared in *The New Yorker*, *Harper's*, and numerous other publications. He directs the Premio Aura Estrada. Every year, he teaches one semester at Trinity College in Hartford, Connecticut, and then hightails it back to Mexico City.

Jewelle Gomez is the author of seven books, including the cult classic black lesbian vampire novel *The Gilda Stories*, whose twenty-fifth anniversary edition was published by City Lights Books. Her adaptation of the novel for the stage, *Bones and Ash*, was performed by Urban Bush Women dance company in thirteen U.S. cities. She is also the author of

Waiting for Giovanni, a play about James Baldwin. Her new play about singer-songwriter Alberta Hunter is called *Leaving the Blues* and premiered at New Conservatory Theatre Center in spring 2017. Follow her at @VampyreVamp and www.jewellegomez.com.

Reyna Grande is the author of three critically acclaimed books: *Across a Hundred Mountains, Dancing with Butterflies,* and *The Distance Between Us.* She has received an American Book Award, the Premio Aztlán Literary Prize, and the Luis Leal Award for Distinction in Chicano/Latino Literature, among others. Born in Iguala, Mexico, Reyna was nine years old when she came to the United States as an undocumented immigrant to be reunited with her father. Through her work, she hopes to put a human face to the controversial issue of immigration. Visit her at www.reynagrande.com to learn more about her.

Born in Syria, **Mohja Kahf** is a professor at the University of Arkansas. She is the author of a novel, *The Girl in the Tangerine Scarf* (2006), and the book of poems *E-mails from Scheherazad.* Her second book of poetry, *Hagar Poems* (2016), treats the story of Hagar, Abraham, and Sarah. She is a member of the Syrian Nonviolence Movement and a Boycott, Divestment, Sanctions Movement supporter.

Katie Kitamura is the author of *Gone to the Forest* and *The Longshot*, both finalists for the New York Public Library's Young Lions Fiction Award. A recipient of a Lannan Foundation Residency Fellowship, Kitamura has written for several publications, including *The New York Times Book Review*, *The Guardian*, *Granta*, *BOMB*, *Triple Canopy*, and *The White Review* and is a regular contributor to *Frieze*. Her third novel, *A Separation*, was published in early 2017.

Born in London, **Hari Kunzru** is the author of the novels *The Impressionist*, *Transmission*, *My Revolutions*, *Gods Without Men*, and *White Tears*, as well as a short story collection, *Noise*, and a novella, *Memory Palace*. He was a 2008 Cullman Fellow at the New York Public Library, a 2014 Guggenheim Fellow, and a 2016 Fellow of the American Academy in Berlin. He lives in New York City.

Chip Livingston is the queer, mixed-blood Creek author of the novel *Owls Don't Have to Mean Death* (2017); an essay collection, *Naming Ceremony*; and two poetry collections, *Crow-Blue*, *Crow-Black* and *Museum of False Starts*. His writing has appeared in *Prairie Schooner*, *Ploughshares*, *South Dakota Review*, and *The Cincinnati Review* and on the Poetry Foundation's and Academy of American Poets' websites. Chip teaches in the low-residency MFA programs at the Institute of American Indian Arts and at Regis University. Visit www.chiplivingston.com.

Claire Messud's *The Emperor's Children* was a *New York Times*, *Los Angeles Times*, and *Washington Post* Best Book of the Year. Her first novel, *When the World Was Steady*, and her book of novellas, *The Hunters*, were both finalists for the PEN/Faulkner Award, and her second novel, *The Last Life*, was a *Publishers Weekly* Best Book of the Year and Editor's Choice at *The Village Voice*. All four books were named *New York Times* Notable Books of the Year. Messud has been awarded Guggenheim and Radcliffe Fellowships and a Strauss Living from the American Academy of Arts and Letters. She lives in Cambridge, Massachusetts, with her husband and children.

Cherríe Moraga is the coeditor of *This Bridge Called My Back: Writings by Radical Women of Color* (with the late Gloria Anzaldúa). She is the author of *A Xicana Codex of Changing Consciousness: Writings 2000–2010* and a new literary memoir entitled *The Native Country of a Heart—A Geography of Desire*. Moraga is the recipient of a USA Rockefeller Fellowship for Literature. She is an artist in residence in theater and performance studies and comparative studies in race and ethnicity at Stanford University. She is a founding member of La Red Xicana Indígena.

Celeste Ng is the author of the novel *Everything I Never Told You*, which was a *New York Times* bestseller, a *New York Times* Notable Book of 2014, and Amazon's #1 Best Book of 2014 and named a best book of the year by more than a dozen publications. *Everything I Never Told You* was also the winner of the Massachusetts Book Award, the Asian/Pacific American Award for Literature, the American Library Association's Alex Award, and the Medici Book Club Prize. Her second novel, *Little Fires Everywhere*, will be published by Penguin Press and Little, Brown UK in fall 2017.

Viet Thanh Nguyen's novel *The Sympathizer* is a *New York Times* bestseller and won the Pulitzer Prize for Fiction.

Other honors include the Dayton Literary Peace Prize, the Edgar Award for Best First Novel, and the Andrew Carnegie Medal for Excellence in Fiction from the American Library Association. His other books are *Nothing Ever Dies: Vietnam and the Memory of War*, a finalist for the National Book Award in nonfiction and a National Book Critics Circle Award; *Race and Resistance: Literature and Politics in Asian America*; and *The Refugees*. He is the Aerol Arnold Chair of English and professor of American studies and ethnicity at the University of Southern California.

Achy Obejas is the author of the forthcoming *The Tower of the Antilles* as well as the critically acclaimed *Ruins* and *Days of Awe*. She edited and translated *Havana Noir*, crime stories by Cuban writers on and off the island. She has translated Junot Díaz, Rita Indiana, Wendy Guerra, and many others. In 2014, she was awarded a USA Ford Fellowship for her writing and translation. She currently serves as the Distinguished Visiting Writer at Mills College in Oakland, California. In 2016, Mills debuted its MFA in translation, which she codirects. For more about Achy, visit her website at www.achyobejas.com.

Peter Orner is the author of the novels *The Second Coming of Mavala Shikongo* and *Love and Shame and Love*, the story collections *Esther Stories* and *Last Car Over the Sagamore Bridge*, and, most recently, the essay collection/memoir *Am I Alone Here?* His fiction and nonfiction have appeared in *The New York Times*, *The Atlantic*, *Granta*, *The Paris Review*, *McSweeney's*, *The Southern Review*, and many other publications. His stories have been anthologized in *The Best American Short Stories* and twice received a Pushcart Prize. Orner has been awarded a Rome Prize, a Guggenheim Fellowship, a two-year Lannan Foundation Literary Fellowship, and a Fulbright to Namibia. He is a professor of creative writing at San Francisco State University.

Roxana Robinson is the author of nine books: five novels, including *Cost*; three collections of short stories; and the biography *Georgia O'Keeffe: A Life*. Her work has appeared in *The New Yorker*, *The Atlantic*, *Harper's*, *The New York Times*, *The Washington Post*, *Bookforum*, *The Best American Short Stories*, *Tin House*, and elsewhere. She teaches in the Hunter MFA program and divides her time among New York, Connecticut, and Maine. She has received fellowships from the National Endowment for the Arts and the Guggenheim Foundation and is the president of the Authors Guild.

Meredith Russo is a transgender writer from Chattanooga, Tennessee. While she mostly reads fantasy and sci-fi, she can't help writing schmaltzy love stories with a side of LGBT (emphasis on the *T*) representation. Her debut novel, *If I Was Your Girl*, tells the story of a transgender girl moving to a small town to live with her estranged father after an assault and her attempts to navigate love, friendship, and truth as the person she was always meant to be. When she isn't writing, Meredith can usually be found yelling about social justice and Japanese cartoons on social media.

Kate Schatz is the *New York Times* bestselling author of *Rad American Women A–Z* and *Rad Women Worldwide*. Her book of fiction, *Rid of Me: A Story*, was published in 2007 as part of the 33¹/₃ series. Her work has been published in *Lenny Letter, BuzzFeed, Signature, Oxford American, East Bay Express*, and *Joyland*, among others. Her short story "Folsom, Survivor" was included as a Notable Short Story in *The Best American Short Stories 2011*. She is a cofounder of Solidarity Sundays, a feminist activist group, and she lives with her family on the island of Alameda, California.

Lisa See is the *New York Times* bestselling author of numerous novels, including *Snow Flower and the Secret Fan, Shanghai Girls*, and *China Dolls*. Her most recent novel, *The Tea Girl of Hummingbird Lane*, was released by Scribner in March 2017. *Booklist* has said of the new novel, "See's focus on the unbreakable bonds between mothers and daughters, by birth and by circumstance, becomes an extraordinary homage to unconditional love." See's books have been published in thirty-nine languages. You can learn more about her at www.lisasee.com.

Jane Smiley is the author of twenty-six works of fiction and nonfiction. She won the Pulitzer Prize in 1992 for *A Thousand Acres*. Her recent trilogy, The Last Hundred Years *(Some Luck, Early Warning, Golden Age)*, won the Heartland Prize. She was raised in Saint Louis, Missouri, lived for a long time in Iowa, and now lives in California. She frequently writes for *The Guardian* and *The New York Times*.

Luis Alberto Urrea is the author of sixteen books, including *The Water Museum*, a finalist for the 2016 PEN/Faulkner Award; *The Devil's Highway*, winner of the Lannan Literary

Award and a finalist for the Pulitzer Prize; and the novel *The Hummingbird's Daughter*, winner of the Kiriyama Prize. Urrea is a member of the Latino Literature Hall of Fame, and his books have been bestsellers and been selected for nearly one hundred city or college One Book, One Community reads. He has also received numerous additional honors, including an Edgar Award, an American Book Award, and a Christopher Award. Urrea lives with his family in Naperville, Illinois, where he is a distinguished professor of creative writing at the University of Illinois at Chicago.

iO Tillett Wright is an artist, activist, actor, speaker, TV host, and writer whose memoir, *Darling Days*, was published in 2016. His work deals with identity, be it through photography in the Self Evident Truths Project / We Are You campaign or on television as the cohost of MTV's *Suspect*. iO has exhibited artwork in New York and Tokyo and was a featured contributor on underground culture to *T: The New York Times Style Magazine*. He has had photography featured in *GQ*, *Elle*, *New York* magazine, and *The New York Times Magazine*. A native New Yorker, iO is now based in Los Angeles.

PERMISSIONS

About the Editor

Carolina De Robertis, a writer of Uruguayan origins, is the author of the novels *The Gods of Tango*, *Perla*, and the international bestseller *The Invisible Mountain*. Her books have been translated into seventeen languages and have been named Best Books of the Year in venues including the *San Francisco Chronicle*; *O, The Oprah Magazine*; *Booklist*; and NBC. She is the recipient of a Stonewall Book Award, Italy's Rhegium Julii Prize, and a fellowship from the National Endowment for the Arts, among other honors. She is also an award winning translator of Latin American literature. A longtime activist, De Robertis spent ten years in the nonprofit sector before publishing her first book, and during that time, she led projects concerning issues including women's rights, immigrant rights, and addressing sexual violence. She teaches creative writing at San Francisco State University and lives in Oakland, California, with her wife and two children.